The Norwayne Tales

Preserving A Heritage

A Narrative Collection
Various Authors

Foreword - Larry Jones,
Norwayne Alumni President

Editors
Van Jewell Sampson Marshall

Sherree Sutton

For information, address Norwayne Alumni and Friends, Inc., 106 East Alumni Way, P.O. Box 1131, Fremont, NC 27830 -1131 or www.norwaynealumni.org.

Foreword by Larry Jones, Norwayne Alumni President.

The *Stories*, referred to as *Narratives*, by people associated with Norwayne Alumni and Friends, Inc. rooted in the North Carolina Wayne County communities of Pikeville, Fremont, and Eureka.

Produced by the Norwayne Storybook Framing Committee: Larry Jones, President; Tony Moore, Vice President; Franklin Coley, Historian; Van Jewell Sampson Marshall and Sherree Sutton, Editors.

| ISBN | 979-8-9866501-2-8 | (hardcover) |
| ISBN | 979-8-9866501-3-5 | (paperback) |

Revised Edition: September 2023
First Edition: September 2022 (Out of Print)

Published by Voice of the Rainbow Publishing (In-Kind; a Work of Love)
Printed in The United States of America

A Piece of History

Original Norwayne School Campus

Image captured from *The Norwaynian 1960*
The Senior Class Yearbook

*Photo reconstruction and back cover
picture courtesy of
Corey O. Coley
Warm Reception Events*

Our
History Continued

When Our Name Was Norwayne School

Our Gym When Our Mascot
was
The Mighty Lion!

Foreword

Life and its many wonders of journeys and of mountains are truly amazing, when you think of *"How Great Thou Art."* It is all put into perspective by those words. We know *"It is not Us but God"* who makes all things possible in all of our journeys. You will never know the journey that any of us traveled until we tell our individual stories. Each of us has one. The purpose of this book is to provide a platform for anyone to tell their story.

I thank the Framing Committee and the authors for all of their work in making these stories available to you and in some special ways come alive in your mind. A special thank you to Van Jewell Sampson Marshall and Sherree Sutton for their extra hard work and dedication to make this vision of a Norwayne book of stories a reality.

You will find these stories to be enlightening, compassionate, motivating, faith driven and each with an *"I will not give up"* spirit. You will find that you can relate to and/or are touched by each one in some way. It is said, every journey starts somewhere with one step at a time.

I find these stories powerful in how the writers overcame the many distractions and noise and how each continued with pure will power and determination not to let failures cause them not to be successful, but rather to develop the can-do attitude and drive and faith to never give up. Even God had challenges with people who failed and, in some cases, had to start over; but He never gave up on us, and when man needed a lifeline, He provided us with Jesus.

We all have mountains to climb and valleys to travel, but our faith will always carry us through as is repeated in these stories.

It is our hope that others will want to share their stories to continue to educate, inspire and remember from whence we came. That same hope is reserved for others associated with *Norwayne Alumni and Friends, Inc.* rooted in the North Carolina Wayne County communities of Pikeville, Fremont, and Eureka. If you do not have a story in this first edition, we hope you will consider contributing to future editions in our effort to *"Go Tell Somebody"* about the great things God has done in our lives. Because, we are all witnesses of His touch.

Iron sharpeneth iron; so a man
sharpeneth the countenance of his friend.   *Proverbs 27:17*

Larry Jones
President, Norwayne Alumni and Friends, Inc.

CONTENTS

Narrators are listed alphabetically (females maiden name first) except the first narrative by Franklin Coley who gives the Norwayne Alma Mater History as prelude to the School Song.

9

11

Introduction

Extraordinary people commonly have extraordinary life experiences. In this book, you will meet some remarkable people as they are introduced through the stories shared here.

Norwayne Alumni & Friends, Inc. (NAFI) is a non-profit founded on the principles of education and community. NAFI is celebrating 50 years of making a difference in the lives of students seeking educational sponsorship and support. Since its inception, NAFI has expanded its focus to include community outreach and the association continues to build out its wheelhouse on a firm foundation - a foundation deeply rooted in the Pikeville, Fremont, and Eureka communities. Present-day community outreach activities include food banks (Food Insecurity Groups and *Lions' Dens* are located at Charles B. Aycock High School, Norwayne Middle School, and Fremont Elementary School. The *Lions' Den* name is an effort to keep the Norwayne Lion name alive and to help others.); mental health and addiction referral services; CPR training certification; clergy outreach; youth-focused projects; and town improvement. The Theme for this year's anniversary is *Celebrating 50 Years: Go Tell Somebody: Luke 8:39*, which coincides with the publishing of *The Norwayne Tales: Preserving A Heritage.*

Culture and heritage are two of the greatest gifts we can convey to the next generation. The stories shared on the pages of this book will serve as the authors' gifts to the reader - current and future generations. Within these pages are stories of love, family, belief, pain, recovery, determination, perseverance, tenacity, and success.

As you read this delightful book, *The Norwayne Tales: Preserving A Heritage,* with its charming language and depictions of personalities and events, we hope that you will not only enjoy the stories but also find yourself immersed in the times and the places.

Each story was followed in detail, as much as possible, including varying linguistic styles.

To preserve the manuscripts' personality, edits were used primarily to improve readability and increase comprehension. This accounts for the varying use of capitalizations, punctuations, positioning of adverbs and adjectives, and other anomalies. All stories, as true and loving works of the authors, were permitted for this publication.

Without any knowledge of what each other was writing, amazingly, *every* one of the twenty-five Narrators, *some* way or *some* how, honored and lifted up *The Most High* in their stories. This Norwayne Story Book Project has turned out to be a book of Praise! Yes, it's time to *Go Tell Somebody*!

In the words of Maya Angelou, *"You can't really know where you are going until you know where you have been."*

The Norwayne Book Framing Committee

Larry Jones, Alumni President
Tony Moore, Alumni Vice President
Franklin Coley, Historian
Van Jewell Sampson Marshall and Sherree Sutton, Editors

Franklin Coley   Norwayne Class of 1964

Dear NORWAYNE School

Mr. Carney called it, *"A Gem of a School Song/Alma Mater."* None of the mouths of the thousands of ears that have heard it ever objected to our icon's proud claim.
Circa 1959, Elementary Music Teacher, Ms. Jean Gaither Hargrove and three select ninth grade students wrote, practiced, polished, and performed our beloved "Alma Mater".

The three Class of 1963 students were: William "Jake" Green (Marva Yelverton Green,'64), Willie Jerome Johnson Evans, and Thomas Roy Carey. The three were amazingly gifted bass, baritone, and tenor Glee Club students. Evans and Carey are deceased. As is Ms. Hargrove.

Ms. Ann Hunt Jones Smith was Norwayne High School Glee Club/ Choral Director, Music Teacher, and Angelic Arrival in 1958-1960. She professionally adopted the cause of the founding four, using her talents and Glee Club to perfect our "Gem of a *Dear NORWAYNE School* Song Alma Mater."

1959-1960*
The musical basis for *Dear NORWAYNE School* is a gospel tune, *"Be Still My Soul."* That work is an adaptation of Finnish composer Jean Sibelius's *"Finlandia*' from his *Symphony #2*.

Ms. Ann Hunt Jones Smith transitioned in June, 2023, before the publication of this Revised Edition. (Her "Unforgettable Memories" story is on page 72.)

15

The Norwayne School Alma Mater

Dear Norwayne School,

O, how we do adore thee!

You've set high goals and standards we must reach;

Our striving will bring merits and success.

Your concepts true, no other school can match.

Teach us to build, Dear Norwayne, lend us sight

to see the towers gleaming in the light.

Oh, Norwayne School,

Our faith and trust in thee

Will guide our feet through paths that we must trod.

We owe our laurels to the Blue and Gold;

Your walls are echoing to us our aims;

We give to you, Dear Norwayne, our devotion.

Dear Alma Mater, how we do adore thee!

Lyrics taken from the Norwayne School Yearbook, *The Norwaynian 1960*

My True Hero

While growing up I thought that heroes had to be a football player, baseball player, or a basketball player. Not realizing these people would be someone I would never meet in life. Yet I wondered and thought, who is my real hero? I understood that my hero was someone who had faith in me, when I felt like giving up. Now with much prayer and many tears, as *I saw the light*, I knew it would not always be this way. Yet still I was searching and looking for my true hero.

Sometimes feeling inferior seeing others with *and* I was without. The feelings and thought that I was poor.

Realizing someone who had more faith than I had said to me, "You are going to make it." I was trying not to be overcome with depression; I must say loudly, that *I did make it!*

Meeting the *Love of my life*. She had a spirit that was unique, very helpful and encouraging. With the ups and downs in life, I *again* did make it!

And, I must say, I found my *True Hero* in life, and it was my grandmother. I remember Grandmother used to get me up early in the morning, boiling water for wash ups, preparing breakfast, and sending me off to school. I can remember her telling me to study smart, and hard.

So again, my true hero was my grandmother, and her name was Bessie L. Coley, and to me she was *Ma Bessie.*

Linda Gail Coley   (Migrated) Brooklyn, NY   Class of 1976

HIDING OUT

I have always wondered how this got into the newspaper. I was missing for less than 24 hours. Without the article above I would not have remembered the date of the incident, but I do remember what had happened that day.

You see what had happened was, we were staying with my cousin Betty (Cuzin Bet) and Cousin Henry on Sycamore Street. Cuzin Bet gave me 11 cents to go to the store to buy some candy (MaryJanes). I go skipping, hopping to Ms. Minnie's store. As you went into the store there was a big gumball machine. I asked for the candy and put a coin in the bubble gum machine and a gumball rolled out. Ms. Minnie has the bag of candy; I go to give her the dime and it's a penny. I had put the dime in the gumball machine by mistake. I tried to tell Ms. Minnie about the mistake, but she wasn't having it or didn't believe it. So, I walked back home to tell Cuzin Bet what had happened.

I got back to the house and told Cuzin Bet what happened; she didn't believe me either. She said, "If you don't go back and get that candy or my money back, I'm going to whoop you." So, I walked back to Ms. Minnie's store crying and pleading with her to give me the candy or the dime back. No such luck. I started to walk back to the house crying and thinking about what to do. I suddenly had an idea: *I'll hide out until Momma gets home from work and she will give me the money and keep Cuzin Bet from whooping me.*

Remember, I said we were living with my cousins; we hadn't been there long. My Momma's furniture was packed up on the back porch. Which wasn't a real back porch, it was closed in on all sides, with a screen at the top of one wall. Anyway, it was daylight when I crawled in between the furniture and fell asleep.

I woke up sometime later and crawled out of my hidey-hole and it was dark outside. I went to the back door that goes into the house. Before I could knock on the door, I heard Tanger, Belinda and Peggy. (Maybe not Peggy so much, but she was there). One of them was saying *"Someone took Gail. I don't know who did it. I think she is dead!!"* And then they begin to cry. All three of them were younger than me. I'm standing on the back porch touching my arms, legs and chest thinking *"I'm not dead, am I?"*

Scared and crying, I crawl back in my hidey-hole and go back to sleep. I woke up later to a lot of noise and loud voices; My Momma was one of those voices. Finally, she was home. I remember walking around the side of the house. There were police cars, a fire truck and an ambulance. It seemed like all the lights were going. I was slightly behind a bush when I was snatched up from behind and the person was saying *"Here she is, here she is."* I don't know who that person

21

was, but Momma grabbed me and hugged me so tight. I don't remember the rest of the night, but the next morning, I remember Momma and I sitting side by side on the couch. I was crying and my Momma was sad. Cuzin Bet told her if she didn't whoop me, she had to move out. She said some other things, I'm sure, but my young brain was stuck on the word "whooping."

Cuzin Bet left the house to get water from the well next door. As she left Momma said, "Keep crying." And she pinched me a couple of times to make me scream louder. She held me tight and said "I'm going to get us out of here; it's just going to take some time. Don't ever do something like that again." When Cuzin Bet got back to the house, she told me years later, *there wasn't a teardrop on my face.*

I was banned from Ms. Minnie's store and told never to go in there again. So, I was really excited when John Coley opened his store. My Momma was one of the ladies that moved out of Fremont in the 1960 leaving us kids with family in the hope of doing better up north.

I'm sure Cuzin Bet got her whooping in over the years that I was in her care. Because I was a busy, always thinking kid. I thought it was magic to go to bed with dirty feet and wake up in the morning and they would be clean. Momma did move us out of that situation, and it did take time. During those years Cuzin Bet became more than a cousin, she became our grandmother. Her house was the place we would always return to during the holidays and summer vacation. She was the person who celebrated our achievements and goals, big and small.

Linda Gail Coley, USMC, Retired FBOP

A Push to Believe

I recollect discovering that I could sing in church, *Morning Star Apostolic Church* in Fremont to be exact. Not that I had any choice, for every child had to sing during the youth programs or help the adult choir. However, my mom would bribe me to sing a duet with my big sister, and after I felt more confident, a solo.

I tried to blend in and sing like the other children, but as I approached puberty, my voice began to take on a unique, operatic tone that did not fit into the loud, boisterous music indicative of the Pentecostal church. So, I hid it.

I would go to my upstairs bedroom and open the window (so I wouldn't disturb my family downstairs) and just sing, sing, sing like a canary. I was dreadfully shy at that age, so imagine the embarrassment I felt when my friend Sheila told me that she could hear me at her house on the corner a block away! In fact, I remember when I stayed overnight with my friend Margie, she begged me to sing for her mother. I reluctantly gave in, only if they'd let me sing behind a closed door! I just felt that no one appreciated that soprano type of tone.

That negative idea about my voice began to change when I met my sister's music teacher, Angelo Holman. Mom could only afford to give one of us piano lessons, so that opportunity went to my big sister, Pat. She told Mister Holman that I could sing and, after her piano lesson at our house, he invited me to learn the song, *Summertime* from the musical **Porgy & Bess**. Well, I had no Idea that I'd impressed him until he sent for me the next day from the *Norwayne Middle School* building where I was in 6ᵗʰ grade, to come to the *Norwayne High School* building and sing *Summertime* for his choir! He was giving me a push to believe that I could sing. I was scared to death when I walked into the gym and looked up into the stands at those older, more mature groups of singers in his choir. As I usually did at the time, I closed my eyes as he played the introduction with such magnificent proficiency and began to sing the song. I prayed that it would all be over soon. When it finally ended and I opened my eyes, I received a standing ovation! I thought to myself, "What, for me? Those notes were so easy!" I walked back to the middle school building with a smile.

Later, Mr. Holman asked me to sing the song in the talent show at the *Wayne County Fair*. I was less afraid to enter the contest because Mr. Holman was a master at playing piano and was sure to make me sound good. So, I was in shock when the program got closer and closer to my name, and there was no Mr. Holman. I prayed that he would get there in time, but to my dismay my name was called. My mom, Jessie Bell Coley, squeezed my hand and told me to go on up. I slowly walked up the steps to the stage and looked into the anxious faces of the crowd of parents and friends who came to watch their children. I took a deep breath and relied on the training I'd had in church when there was no music. I closed my eyes and sang from my heart. My voice rang out and echoed from the roof of the metal building. It was so quiet; you could hear a pin drop! When I finished, I was so glad it was over until I didn't stay for the results, after all, I had no accompaniment! I concentrated on getting on my favorite rides and bought my favorite food rather than think about my awful performance. I had to stand flat footed and sing raw before all those people, when the beautiful embellishments of my teacher's piano playing would have added so much more! Eventually I went back to join my mother at the talent show building.

I was so surprised when my mother met me with her face beaming and waving something in her hand. She said, "You won first place! You weren't here when they called your name and I had to receive it for you. I was so nervous until I said, "I'm her daughter". (Of course, she meant to say "I'm her mother.")

As I remember those moments, I'm in tears. I never knew I had a gift until then. I sang the same song after integration, in the *Charles B Aycock* pageant, though I didn't place there. But I sang it in the *Zeta Phi Beta* sponsored *Miss Wayne County Pageant* and won! My confidence grew and I sang it in college to win 2nd place as *Miss JCSU.* Later, I would follow Mr. Holman's footsteps and become a music teacher myself. Because of him, I was careful to look for gifts in students and do everything I could to expose them and give them experiences in music they would not have had otherwise. I'm proud of the 35 years that I taught and I'm confident that I have passed on the torch and helped push someone else to believe in their God-given gifts!

Old Set Me Free

I was an avid reader. I used to read a lot to escape the boredom of a strict upbringing. You see we couldn't go outside our yard to play, or risk being sent to get your own switch by Big Mama. Big Mama (also known as Mother Odessa McKinnon) was my grandmother. My mom (Jessie Bell Coley) moved our family comprised of my mom, my two sisters, Juanita and LaVone and me from Goldsboro, NC to Fremont, NC to live with Big Mama after her husband, our grandfather, died. I felt like a fish out of water. Everything changed…Big Mama's rules applied now. I went from a happy go lucky kid, to what I thought felt like imprisonment. We even had to turn the TV off if Big Mama walked in the room. So, I started reading a lot.

When we moved to Fremont from Goldsboro, I was in the second grade. I was enrolled in Friendship Elementary School. In the third grade, I went from Friendship Elementary School to Norwayne. Norwayne had grades 3-12. I was challenged by my Norwayne elementary teacher, Ms. Graham, to read, pay attention, and participate or get my ears pulled. Boy would that hurt, -but it worked. I believe pulling ears today would be considered child abuse. My eighth-grade teacher, Ms. Harris, told me that I would never amount to anything. This was countered by my favorite teacher, Mr. Angelo Holman, to be the best I could be. "If you are going to be a pea counter, you count those peas right. So, when they get a bag with your name on it, they will know they are counted right."

This statement by Mr. Holman became my mantra. I tried to do my best in everything I did at Norwayne. Whether it was in class. Whether it was in the choir. Whether it was as a cheerleader. Whether it was in band. I always tried to do and be my best. I was so intent on doing my best that I decided to go to Charles B. Aycock High School my freshman year.

You see, Norwayne's new books used to have Charles B. Aycock stamped in them when the students at Norwayne received the books as "new." I didn't want the old books. I wanted the books when they were fresh off the press - new. So, in September 1965, I was one of seventeen Black students enrolled at Charles B. Aycock under the Freedom of Choice plan.

The Freedom of Choice plan gave you the opportunity to voluntarily go to Charles B. Aycock in Pikeville, NC. My motivation was not out of civic pride, I just wanted the books when they were new. My God, did I regret this move.

First of all, several of us had to walk from Fremont to Pikeville along the railroad track to school. This was because there was not a bus that came in my neighborhood on its way to the all-White Charles B. Aycock High School. As if these three miles, one-way, walks were not bad enough, I had to deal with the White students throwing bottles, sticks, paper---whatever they could find to throw at us.

The experience of racial abuse at Charles B. Aycock opened my eyes to the wonderful years I had left behind at Norwayne. I began to see and appreciate my old school in a brand-new light. At Norwayne I felt empowered, loved, valued, and appreciated. I was recognized for my gifts and challenged to do better in areas that needed improvement.

At Charles B. Aycock, the teacher reluctantly had to be my partner in PE activities that required two people. None of the White students dared touch me lest the black would rub off me onto them. In the classroom, chairs were empty all around me because the White students didn't want to sit near me. Teachers seemed amazed that I could read. Walking down the hall, passage was often blocked so I would have to hear the n-word jokes being told as the students threw their heads back with laughter while clapping their hands. I had had enough, so I told my father.

My father, James R. Walker, Jr., was an attorney. All I know is that he came to Charles B. Aycock school with me one day - legal pad in one hand - holding my hand with the other hand. We went to Principal Donald Jones' office. My dad asked me to wait outside the office. I don't know what was written on that pad or what my dad said to Mr. Jones; but I do know that all of a sudden, I was treated differently.

The principals at Norwayne and Charles B. Aycock got together making it possible for me to ride a Norwayne bus that came by my house. The Norwayne bus would drop me off at Charles B. Aycock while en route to Norwayne. I no longer had to walk to school or get picked up after school by my mother.

Principal Jones must have had a meeting with all the teachers and the White students because I received "special" treatment. Needless to say, this did not go over too well with my Black brothers and sisters.

Old set me free. My sophomore year, I hurriedly returned to my old school, Norwayne, where I graduated with honors. The mantra Mr. Holman instilled in me gave me the courage to excel. I went to college and graduate school, receiving a bachelor and two master's degrees. My career included working for Burroughs Corporation (now Unisys), CBS headquarters in New York, managing fifteen radio stations for Greater Media Inc., owning my own Public Relations firm, and training senior executives for the Federal Aviation Administration and Social Security Administration. Additionally, I was a pastor in the AME church in Jacksonville, Florida. I am now retired. I am raising my eleven-year-old grandson, Kendrick Marja Burton Tran, while being actively involved in my church and community. I believe a great deal of my success can be attributed to God, my family, friends, and of course, Norwayne School.

When God Steps In

Divine intervention, by definition, is when God steps in and changes the outcome of a situation. My interpretation, however, is when God puts you in the right place at the right time to fulfill His ultimate plan. In my short 30 years of life, I recall two distinct instances where God put me in the right place at just the right time in order to be there for certain people that I loved.

My first flashback goes to April 24, 2006, the day after my fifteenth birthday. Like any typical school day, I would ride the bus on my way home from school. At the time my then 89-year-old grandmother was still living with my mom and me, so I was never alone when I got home. Now typically, my neighbor and I were always the last two students to get off on my bus driver's route so we would normally get home around 4:30 PM; sometimes (and I could count on one hand how many times it occurred) he would reverse the route and allow us to be some of the first students to get home. This particular day, April 24th, was one of those days my bus driver decided to drop me off at the beginning of the route. As we made our way around the curve on my road, in the distance I could see lights from a firetruck, an ambulance, and several cars all parked in front of my house. As we got closer and closer, in the back of my mind I was just hoping that it was a minor car accident that happened, however, when we got as close as we could to my house, I saw a man closing the front door. I rushed off the bus and saw them wheeling my grandma on a stretcher into the ambulance. When I ran up to the EMT, he informed me that my grandma had been involved in an accident and was struck by a vehicle while walking to the mailbox.

Thankfully she was alert and was talking to the EMTs in her full state of mind, but unfortunately, I now had the daunting task of calling my mom at work and telling her what happened. My mom quickly rushed home to pick me up and we went to the hospital to be with my grandma. Although she passed away three days later, we thank God that she was not taken instantly, and we were able to spend time with her while she was in a good state of mind. My biggest takeaway from this experience was that of my definition of divine intervention – God put me in the right place at the right time. If my bus driver had taken his normal route that day, I would have come home to an empty house unaware of what had happened to my grandma; He placed me right where I needed to be.

Fast forward years later to September 10, 2019. This would be my second instance of God placing me where I was desperately needed. This was one of the happiest seasons of my life – I was preparing for my wedding day in just 32 short days. At this certain point in time, I had just transferred to Johnston County Schools since I would soon be moving to Clayton and my school was approximately 50 minutes from home (Fremont). During this time of my life, my father had also been battling multiple myeloma for several years and was currently on dialysis three days a week. I made it a point to call my dad every day to check on him, but on September 10th, God intervened when my dad needed me the most. Ironically, I was scheduled to take my bridal portraits that day at my venue in Greenville, NC. My mom accompanied me that day and it started with my makeup appointment first thing that morning followed by a hair appointment. While I was getting my hair done, I received a call from my dad's dialysis center that he had not shown up for his dialysis session which was certainly uncommon for him. I then tried to call him several times myself and was unable to reach him. After getting my hair done, my mom and I were on the way to Greenville on I-795 and I continued trying to reach my dad. As we were approaching the Fremont exit, I asked my mom if I should go check on him just to make sure everything was okay, and she agreed that I should. Even though we had to be in Greenville in less than an hour, I knew that my dad took precedence over my bridal portraits. When we arrived at his house, we noticed his car was still in the driveway and the front door was still closed. We approached the door and knocked but he did not answer. I tried calling his cell phone again and I could hear it ringing from outside but still no answer. After several more attempts at calling and knocking, we called the police department to see if they could send someone to his house because I did not have a key to get in. Once the policeman arrived, he made a forceful entry, and I was confronted with one of the most painful moments of my life – my dad had passed away.

They say hindsight is 20/20 and although I selfishly wanted my dad to live long enough to enjoy the moment of him walking me down the aisle, it was his time to be with the Lord. I now see that God, again, put me in the right place at the right time. On any other ordinary day, I would have been 50 minutes to an hour away at work and it would have taken me longer to get to him, however, God intervened and orchestrated the events of that day to allow me to be right where I needed to be.

Event though we may not understand why things happen the way they do at that certain time, God will make His plans clear to His people. These two instances have shown me that God is real, and He allowed me to be where I needed to be. These experiences were not just a coincidence but God's divine intervention in my life.

Rev MacArthur Edmundson, Th.D.

Charles B. Aycock   Class of 1979

Spoken Words Caused a Life-Altering Experience

MacArthur Edmundson was born and raised in Fremont, North Carolina. After graduating from high school, he entered the U.S. Army. Mac spent 26 years on active duty and retired as a Command Sergeant Major. During his last combat tour in Iraq from December 2003 to December 2004 as the Battalion Command Sergeant Major, he also assisted the Battalion Chaplain in preaching the gospel each Sunday to the Engineer soldiers scattered throughout Iraq. Throughout the entire combat tour, Mac spent most of his time as a prayer warrior and intercessor. As a direct result of prayer, he has seen the hand of God move on five occasions while he was a convoy commander; two wood line ambushes and three roadside bombs. In each incident, no one was hurt or harmed. He is married to the formal Shirley Forte; she is also a native of Fremont, NC. They have two children and three grandchildren. They currently reside in Fayetteville, NC. While in the military, he continued and focused on his education. He is a graduate of Webster University in St. Louis, Missouri, with a Master of Arts in Human Resources Development and Management. He also is a graduate of International Seminary in Plymouth, Florida, with a Doctor of Theology.

Mac Edmundson accepted the Lord Jesus as his savior in August 1982. He was ordained and licensed as a minister under J. L. Sanders Evangelistic Association in Jacksonville, Arkansas, in June 1993. He has served the Lord in different churches/denominations and various positions such as an usher, church treasurer, deacon, Sunday School Teacher, Associate Pastor, Circuit Pastor, and Pastor for a short time while in the military at Fort Polk, Louisiana. While attending Harvest Family Church in Fayetteville, NC, and serving under Bishop and Pastor Rosa Herman, he participated in the church prayer school. Afterward, he became a church prayer team member, where he actively became a prayer warrior. Mac and his family are currently members of Beauty Spot Missionary Baptist Church in Fayetteville, North Carolina, where Rev. Dr. Taijuan O. Fuller is their Senior Pastor. Mac is now on the ministerial team, the Assistant Chairman of the Men's Ministry, and the assistant New Members Orientation Coordinator. Lastly, he is presently retired from the workforce and enjoying his time as a husband, father, and grandfather. He loves the Lord and God's people, he is saved, Spirit-filled, and he is thoroughly convinced that the Lord has called him as an Evangelist to proclaim the end-time message of our Lord and Savior Jesus Christ.

Spoken Words: I was the ninth child of ten born from Willie Ed and Helen Edmundson of Fremont, North Carolina. At eleven years old, I remember this event as if it were a few weeks ago – I went to my grandmother, Mrs. Eva Edmundson's (we call her Mama Eva) house one summer evening. Mama Eva was a devout Christian and a holy woman of God. After I entered her house and sat down, for some reason, I started crying. She asked me what was wrong, and I told her that I almost got into a fight. She then said, "What do you mean that you almost got into a fight?"
I said, "Well, I wanted to fight this boy on the basketball court, but my brother Larry came up and broke us up before we could start fighting."
        Mama Eva then said, "You don't have any business fighting anyway." Then she asked me to come and sit beside her, and she gently placed her right hand on my left hand. Mama Eva was blind, but she had several of the Gifts of the Spirit actively working in her life. For example, the Word of Knowledge and the Word Wisdom was actively present during our brief conversation. She told me that I would be different from all my other brothers and sisters because I would go places that they would only read about in books. She also said, "Everywhere that you go, you will help many people."

I joined the military when I was eighteen years old, and God used my twenty-six years of military service to fulfill the spoken words of my grandmother. Just as she prophesied when I was eleven years old, I have traveled to four different continents and a significant part of the United States.

Spoken Words: Four out of the ten of my mother and father's children graduated from high school. During my junior high school years, I did not have the drive or motivation to continue to high school and graduate. At the time, I had made up my mind that I would drop out of school as soon as I turned sixteen. In 1976, about mid-year of my ninth-grade class, a strange thing happened that I will never forget. Shortly after our school lunch break, I stood alone on the sidewalk at the rear of the gym, watching my classmates go to various places during our lunch break. Briefly, I thought that I would drop out of school as soon as I turned sixteen. Shockingly, no sooner than I could get that thought out of my mind, the assistant principal, Mr. John Kirk, came from behind and touched me on my right shoulder and said, "Young man, do not drop out of school – you have so much in life to look forward to." I turned and looked at him in his eyes in unbelief that he knew what I was thinking about. Mr. Kirk said it again, "Do not drop out of school," and he walked away. From that encounter with the assistant principal, I never thought about dropping out of school again.

However, from that day forward, my perspective on education changed. From the middle of the ninth grade to the end of that school year, my grades went from all "Ds" to "Cs" and "Bs." During my entire three years in high school at Charles B. Aycock, I was an A/B student. This transformation took place in my life because of the words spoken to me by the assistant principal at Norwayne Junior High School.

Spoken Words: By way of the military, I was the first to go to college in my family after completing two assignments as a First Sergeant - the first at Fort Benning, Georgia, and the second in Korea.

In 1998, the Army selected me to work as a Reserve Officers' Training Corps (ROTC) instructor at James Madison University in Harrisonburg, Virginia. ROTC is a group of college and university-based officer training programs for training commissioned officers of the United States Armed Forces. At James Madison University, our ROTC department was under the Sociology Department. As the senior Noncommissioned Officer in our ROTC department, my job consisted of teaching military science subjects and our program's physical fitness/training portion. Our physical fitness program was conducted on Monday, Wednesday, and Friday from 5:30 – 6:30 a.m. We usually had about thirty to forty cadets each semester in the Military Physical Fitness Course. One morning, I noticed this older gentleman participating in our training – I did not know who he was. However, after the training session, he walked up to me, shook my hand, and said, "This was a great physical training session, Sergeant." I soon found out that he was Dr. John Gilge, the Dean of the Sociology Department.

Dr. Gilge became a regular attendee at our physical fitness training, and at the end of each training session, he would walk up to me, shake my hand, and tell me that this was a great physical fitness training session. Later that semester, Dr. Gilge came over to our ROTC department and talked with all the military science instructors. At the end of his briefing, he stayed a little longer and talked with Lieutenant Colonel Daniel Humphery, the ROTC Battalion Commander/Department Head. Afterward, Dr. Gilge came and sat beside me at my table. He started his conversation by saying, "I understand that you will be completing your bachelor degree in a few more semesters. You are a great instructor, and you should continue with your education and complete a master's degree and then go on to complete a doctoral degree." He then looked at me in my eyes and said, " I am serious – you have great potential."

Dr. Gilge spoke and planted a seed of hope in my spirit on that day. In 2000, I was selected to attend the United States Army Sergeants Major Academy at Fort Bliss, Texas, as my next military assignment. While at the academy, I enrolled in the Master of Arts

(Human Resource Development) at Webster University. In 2001, I was selected to go to Fort Leonard Wood, Missouri, as my follow-on assignment after graduating from the Sergeants Major Academy. At Fort Leonard Wood, Missouri, I enrolled again at Webster University and completed my Master's Degree. At the time, completing a bachelor's degree at James Madison University was a significant milestone in my career; however, completing a master's degree was a huge accomplishment. I can trace my encouragement to the spoken word from Dr. John Gilge.

Spoken Word: In October 2020, after completing my Doctoral Dissertation and during my Oral Defense, my mentor, Dr. Joy Abraham from International Seminary in Plymouth, Florida, suggested that I revise my dissertation and convert it into a book. At that time, my focus was to complete the Doctoral Program and graduate, so with a short pause, I told him that I would pray and consider it later. My Doctoral Dissertation consists of seventeen chapters about prayer and miracles performed by Jesus. Six months after completing my academic program, I thought about the conversation Dr. Abraham, my academic advisor, and I had during My Doctoral Oral Defense regarding me writing a book from my Doctoral Dissertation. On that same night, I googled, "how do you publish a book." To my surprise, the following day, three publishing companies contacted me regarding publishing a book. However, one of the three companies called me directly and requested a 45-minute phone interview about my book information. I agreed to the discussion, but I scheduled it a week from the date of our initial phone call. During that week, I selected and arranged the twelve chapters from my Doctoral Dissertation; revised the introduction to correspond with the selected twelve chapters; revised a conclusion to correspond with the chapters; updated my bibliography; and developed my book contents/index.

A week later, during our phone interview, the representative from Author House Publishing in Bloomington, Indiana, gave me a briefing on her company's services and the procedure for publishing a book. After selecting the publishing package and agreeing to the contract, she emailed a list of five items the company needed to publish my book. Since I recently completed my Doctoral Dissertation, the major item of writing and editing the manuscript was already done, and the other things I finished the week prior. After I submitted all the required items and paid the fee for the publishing package, within three weeks, my book was ready for review and sent for printing. I would have never considered writing a book until my academy mentor, Dr. Joy Abraham, suggested that I convert my Doctoral Dissertation into a book. His spoken words directly contributed to me writing "**Praying Effectually: Praying Based on God's Word.**"

In conclusion, many people have spoken powerful words that have become part of my spirit throughout my life. Those words initially took the form similarly as a seed and grew to flourish at the fullness of time. Amazingly, these individuals spoke words that caused me to have life-altering experiences. As noted, my grandmother told me when I was eleven years old that I would travel throughout the world and go places only my sisters and brothers would read about. Also, Mr. John Kirk, the Norwayne Junior High School assistant principal, changed my mind about dropping out of high school and my outlook about school in general by telling me, "Young man, do not drop out of school. You have so much in life to look forward to." Dr. John Gilge, the Dean of the Sociology Department at James Madison University, said, "You are a great instructor, and you should continue with your education and complete a master's degree and then go on to complete a doctoral degree." Lastly, Dr. Joy Abraham, Academy Professor at International Seminary and my academy mentor said, "Your Doctoral Dissertation was well written in a way that would encourage readers. I suggest that you revise your doctoral dissertation and convert it into a book."

These spoken words caused life-altering experiences that became a reality.

My Story

My name is Ida Mae Fleming. Fifth child of some amazing sisters who I thought I would never live up to, as the accomplished women they are. My story begins at Norwayne School in 1968. I was in the first grade and my teacher was Ms. PB Williams. I was a very large girl, so I got picked on all the time. My childhood was devastating to my self-esteem. I was always the largest in my class. When I rode the school bus, I sat alone. My books would be pushed out of the seat. I would be tripped going to my seat. Needless to say, I kept to myself. Well, Ms. PB Williams discovered I could sing just like my sisters. This started me singing at every important assembly in the gym. I felt special. Still picked on, but I had other students who respected my gift, and took up for me.

Well speeding to junior high, I had to make a name for myself. So, I was one of 3 girls who applied to drive the school bus for the school. When I went to bus training, I was the only girl. I had never driven a "stick shift." I was the first to drive, so all the guys in the back were holding their necks saying they were going to have whiplash. I made the cut. My own father (Douglas Lee Fleming) consoled me the night I told him I was getting my own bus route. He said, "I don't want you to be disappointed." I came home that next day with not one bus route, but two routes. One for the Elementary school and one for High school.

The struggle did not end there. I started caring for elderly women in my community. I was good at it. You see I knew at an early age I was called to be a nurse. I did nursing things (*as I shudder*) way before I had license to do it. I said, "Lord, I know this is my calling, how do I get a degree for it, and get paid as well?" So, I looked into Nursing Schools in the area. I shared with my guidance counselor that I wanted to be a nurse. I did my research. The number one Nursing school in the country was at the University of NC in Greensboro

(UNCG). I told my counselor that I was going to apply to this school. She told me, "You know you have a learning disability?" She shared with me from my files that I had been labeled as such. I was crushed. I never knew that label was upon my head. After a couple of days, I returned to her, and said, I am going to UNCG and I am going to be a Registered Nurse. She consoled me, just like my dad. This made me determined, and I applied to UNCG and nowhere else.

Because I have test anxiety, my SAT scores were low. My counselor also shared this with me, as I waited to hear from UNCG. Well, I got my acceptance letter from UNCG. Learned that they had an interim program for people whose SATs were lower than their requirements. They put me in with others who had similar scores to mine. I was making A's on my papers, and tests, and they moved me in the regular flow of students. Thus, my journey as a nurse had begun.

Hurrying to my sophomore year, I applied to the School of Nursing, the struggle is more real. My counselor there at UNCG, told me I was not going to make it. She said, I had enough education to be a LPN, and work my way up. I went to the Dean and changed counselors and shared what she said to me. The Dean was appalled. She sent me to Nancy Fleming Courts. I will never forget her. She thought we were related, so she pulled out the stops for me before she ever met me. She was White, I am Black. We laughed and my journey began again, with her. Long story short, she mentored me to increase my grade point average to a 3.3 to get into the School of Nursing at UNCG.

I graduated from UNCG as a RN in 1987, with a second Major in Community Health Ed. I graduated from Duke University Master's program of Nursing with a Nurse Practitioner's degree 2001; Completed Legal Nurse consulting from Duke University 2013; Certified RN Case Manager of Duke University 2017. I retired from Duke University as a Registered Nurse in 2018. At present, I am a Certified RN Case Manager at WakeMed Raleigh Hospital. Long story short. You can do whatever you set your mind and heart's calling to do. Let no one and nothing stop you from your purpose.

From Disgrace To Grace...
If It Had Not Been

Oh my, where do I start? Let's just start at the beginning when I was a sixteen (16) year-old-unwed-mother and Principal, Mr. J.H. Carney and my English Teacher, Mrs. Olivia West took me under their wings.

Back in the day, which is during the era of the 60's, an unwed mother was frowned upon and considered an absolute "disgrace" to the community, the family, and the school. In the sixties, the rule was if you got pregnant in school you were expelled, put down, and treated like an outcast. Any other principal would have forbidden me to return to "his" school. Remember, this was back in the 60's. Now, this would be unheard of in 2021 and would be labeled discrimination and unfair treatment.

Nevertheless, I was very determined to make something out of my life, more importantly, determined to graduate from high school with my class. If it had not been for Mr. Carney, Mrs. West, my classmates and my parents, Douglas and Ida Hill Fleming, it would have been an impossible task.

How did I do it!? When I knew my pregnancy was a known fact, I voluntarily dropped out of school, therefore, avoided a suspension. If it had not been... My classmates visited me every Sunday to bring work and homework to make sure I completed the first quarter of the 11th grade. I missed the entire second quarter of my junior year.

Now, it is the summer of 1964. I called Mr. Carney to get permission to return to school and to take two English Classes in my 12th year. These English classes were required for me to graduate with my senior class. He and Mrs. West approved both classes; and the rest, as they say, is history.

Guess what, June 1, 1965, not only did I graduate with my senior class, but I also graduated with honor and ranked fourth!

This is not where the story ends... I went on to attend North Carolina College; graduating June 1, 1969, with a B.S. Degree in Commerce with a Minor in Education. Twenty days later, I married the love of my life, my high school sweetheart, Douglas Brown. We have two children, Vanessa, Karen and two grandchildren, Mikayla and Paris.

The story continues... We moved to Washington, D.C. where I began my professional career as a GS-4, Clerk Typist for the Department of State. My career spanned 25 years. During this time, I served in numerous capacities, in the Department of State, e.g., Conference Assistant, Travel Assistant, Procurement Officer. Finally at the age of 47, I retired as a Budget Analyst, October 14, 1994.

The story continues ... In November of 1994, I embarked on a new career. I am still, after 27 years, a Substitute Teacher at Kingsford Elementary, Prince George's County Public Schools, MD.

The end of this story for now... Who would have thought a 16-year old unwed mother in the sixties would have: 1) finished high school; 2) completed college; 3) experienced a successful 25-year tenure with a Federal government agency; 4) served a 27-year second career in teaching; 5) had a 52-year successful marriage; and 6) last but not least, on April 8th 1974, I received Jesus Christ as my personal Savior.

And one more thing I forgot to mention... The child that was born, Vanessa, to this unwed mother was a blessing from God. She grew up and was chosen, at 16, to be a lead soprano in our family group named "The Fleming Sisters" (the late Catherine F. Uzzell, Geraldine

F. Harper, Ethelene F. Reid and Ida Mae Fleming). I sing alto in the group which has produced eight gospel recordings entitled: "Waiting Through The Dark Clouds; "Here I Am Again Lord"; "Hold On"; "Thank You For The Shelter"; "Christmas At Home With The Fleming Sisters"; "Lord You've Done It For Me Again", "Sho' Nuff" and "God If You Help Me".

If it had not been for the "grace" of God, and the people aforementioned, it would have easily been a "total disgrace."

I am living proof, you can, with God on your side, go "From Disgrace to Grace!"

The Other Side of *Through*

"You really need to get that looked at by a doctor," said my dermatologist whom I was seeing for a skin condition in December 2005. He was referring to a large swelling behind my right ear. "It could be something serious," he continued. "Ignoring something unusual because it is not painful can be a big mistake."

I listened and followed through by going to Urgent Care. I was ultimately sent to an ENT doctor in Greenville who performed a biopsy on the lump.

While I waited for the results, my history with lumps, masses, and swellings flashed into my mind. At various times in the past, I have had a lump in my right breast, a lump in my left breast, another lump in my right breast, all of which had been removed, biopsied, and found to be benign. When I was in my forties, one doctor discovered a mass under my right arm which turned out to be a lipoma, a non-cancerous growth of fatty tissue. A few years later, a swelling on my neck, just below my hairline, was removed, biopsied, and found to be non-cancerous. So, I prayed that this time, the results would be the same - no cancer - just a benign mass.

However, when I returned to the doctor's office for the results, he very calmly talked on and on about what he had discovered—and what he had not—yet. He said, "The biopsy results are inconclusive. You have some type of lymphoma, probably non-Hodgkin's. I'm almost sure of that, but I am sending a sample to a lab in Texas...because I did find malignant lymph nodes..."

Malignant?

I didn't clearly decipher anything else he said after the word "malignant." As he continued to explain, I remember thinking about

43

how true the words of Betty Rollins, an NBC news correspondent in the 1970's, were in a book titled *First, You Cry*. She relates how it felt to her when her doctor told her she had breast cancer. To Betty, the news was ultra-shocking; as healthy as she was, how could she possibly have cancer? To me? I had always been so careful, catching every lump, mass, swelling, or bump—always having each one checked out by a doctor. And in the past, none of them had ever been cancerous—until now. I knew God had my back; hadn't He always in the past? But I didn't know what His plans were for me this time.

After all, I had a very dear friend, "Barbara Anne," who died of lymphoma in 2003. Michelle Obama has talked about her best friend while they were both students at Princeton University dying at age 26 from lymphoma. Her name was Michele Alele. The doctor had poured out a jigsaw puzzle of many words, but all I could piece together was, "YOU - HAVE- CANCER!"

And so, I cried.

The ENT doctor referred me to my present oncologist. After more examinations and test results returned, my oncologist told me that I definitely had non-Hodgkin's lymphoma, that it was fast-growing, aggressive, but sometimes those are easiest to treat. He also told me the cancer had spread to my liver and spleen, but he was confident "we" could beat this thing. In dealing with him, my husband Ken and I found out that he believed in God and prayer. That was a plus for us.

Dazed, dismayed, and disappointed, I prayed and hinted to God what He knew already: that I really expected this cancer test to have the same results as all the others had, that He could have made the results negative, and that He had not even given me a clue as to what I was going to be facing.

Then, this revelation unfolded before me:
I envisioned myself at the base of a broad, steep structure which resembled a mountain, around which I could not see. It seemed to be miles wide and miles high, too steep, and slippery to even think about climbing. As I faced it, assessing it, I could feel God's presence. He

was indicating to me, more so than saying, "This is something you must deal with. In the past, I have removed your obstacles; it's different this time."

In other words, I had to get to the other side of that "mountain" by going through it: I couldn't go around it—not this time. God would not remove it – not this time! And then the words, "…Lo, I am with you alway, even unto the end of the world" (Matthew 28:20 KJV) came to mind; and I knew, at that moment, that, with His help, I was going to fight my way through this cancer and live!

Tests revealed that the lymphoma was present on both sides of my face, just under and behind both my ears; in both my armpits; on both sides of my groin area; and on my liver and spleen. Having read stories about people having liver cancer and not surviving caused me some apprehension. Telling people about how I discovered the lymphoma and asking people to pray for me I did readily; but I could not bring myself to tell anyone, not even my children, that the cancer had spread to my liver and spleen. Every time I thought about saying the words, I'd choke up and start to cry. So, I did not say those words; instead, I'd say to myself, "Keep the faith."

I also started reading about the four stages of cancer. I found out that the more widespread the cancer is over the body, the higher the stage number. With lymphoma from my face down to the bottom of my body per se, I refused to read the words confirming that I was in Stage 4, so I closed the book and never finished reading that particular article. I reminded myself that God, not survey results, was in charge of my life.

I started chemotherapy in May of 2006. My oncologist ordered infusions of a drug called Rituxan each time I had the chemotherapy; so, my sessions, which were every three weeks, lasted about five and a half hours. My sessions were all scheduled for Mondays, but the first session started on a Friday with only a 3-hour run of Rituxan. Immediately after the Rituxan run, I felt fine, but in less than thirty minutes after, I had a panic attack such as I had never experienced before. Ken and I had left the doctor's office and stopped at a nearby pharmacy to get some Tylenol tablets. The attack occurred just after he went into the store to get them. Suddenly, I broke out in a cold sweat; I felt disoriented; I remember opening the car door, attempting to get out; but standing was impossible, so I sat back down, but sitting caused me jitters. Breathing was becoming a problem, and I felt nauseous. "Lord, am I going to die right now?" I wondered.

A woman who pulled up and parked right beside our car must have seen my anguish. She told the man who was headed toward our car that something was wrong with his wife. By the time Ken jumped into the car and drove me back to my oncologist's office, the attack was over. Though horrible and debilitating, it lasted only about five minutes. After that first time, I had no more panic attacks with the Rituxan.

The following Monday, I went in for my first chemotherapy session, and a pattern was established: Three hours after I'd finished chemotherapy, I would feel so nauseous that I could not eat, nor could I tolerate the smell of food. So, I would go to bed when I'd get home from my sessions with a quart of water on my nightstand to sip throughout the evening hours. The next morning, I'd get up, take prednisone with a small breakfast, and go about my day as I normally would before I was diagnosed.

Three weeks after my first round of chemo, my hair started falling out. Taking control of a situation over which, I had little control, I asked my husband to cut the rest of my hair off and shave my head before it just fell out. He did. I wasn't about to let lymphoma win every battle!

Four months after my first chemotherapy session, a PET scan declared me cancer-free! My oncologist wanted me to take two more treatments, he said, "just to be sure" it was all completely gone. I complied, of course. By then, it was the end of September 2006.

The journey begun in December of 2005 took me ten months to

complete. During those months, I had experiences I never would have imagined. For example, almost every night while I was taking the chemotherapy drugs, an unidentifiable tune from the 60's played in my dreams…over and over again. Another example was, after each session of chemo, I felt so nauseous, but never vomited—until the very last session, and then, I threw up, and threw up for so long it seemed like I'd never stop.

When that was over, I felt exhausted and wanted to rest. Just before drifting off to sleep, I reviewed my situation: "I took my last treatment today. I am tired, and I'll have to visit an oncologist for the rest of my life but, hey, I am cancer-free! How great is that?"

Yes, the journey was tedious, but God's Word is true: Victory was waiting for me on the other side of *Through*!

Franchesca Tennille Harper
Norwayne Alumni Scholarship Recipient

An Unexpected Homecoming: The Joy Found in the Journey

I dedicate this to all of my family who are members and/or attended schools associated with Norwayne Alumni and Friends, those both living and those who live in our memories.

Part 1:

I'm sure you read the title of this and probably had a memory of the amazing homecoming celebrations you may have attended through the years. I grew up in Greensboro, home of NC A & T, and my mother is a Bennett Belle (just across the street from Aggieland) so GHOE (Greatest Homecoming On Earth!) set the standard for me since I was a little girl. I've been known to go mingle with the Eagles with my aunt/godmother and cousins at NCCU. Even now, as an adult, I'm super excited for "homecoming season" (yes, even for my predominately White alma mater, NC State, GO PACK!) because it's usually on or near my birthday in early November. I worked at the birthplace of "Black Girl Magic," Spelman College for 4 years, so I got to work behind the scenes, understanding the planning that starts the year before for an HBCU homecoming. (And between you, me and this storybook page, SPEL-HOUSE homecoming (with Morehouse) is waaaay better than GHOE but don't tell my brother-in-law or nephew I said that, ok?) Both of my parents, my maternal grandmother and several of my aunts, uncles, and cousins on both sides of the family are lifetime members of the Norwayne Alumni and I remember attending my first banquet in 1989 for my mother's 20th reunion. My paternal grandmother also was on the cafeteria staff when it was a junior high/middle school, so when it comes to Norwayne, the connections are strong and run deep in my roots. Now allow me to introduce myself and tell you how the "homecoming" I had in 2011 wasn't planned. It was devastating and unexpected. There were no fuzzy feelings. My life was turned upside down but there was still joy in the journey…

My name is Franchesca Tennille Harper. Although I did not attend high school in Wayne County, I am a third generation (of 4) current member of the Norwayne Alumni. I'm a 1994 Norwayne Scholarship recipient, as well as a winner of the J.H. Carney Academic Award in that same year. (An honor I cherish and was blessed to meet him on several occasions). My parents are Wilbert Harper, Sr. (class of 1967) and Geraldine Fleming Harper (Class of 1969). My nonagenarian grandmothers, (which I affectionately refer to) are Georgia Lee (93) and Ida B (92, who is a lifetime member of the alumni). Both my niece and nephew are college students that received scholarships and my nephew is a member of the association as well. If you've been paying attention and put it all together, yes, I am one of the Fleming Sisters' daughters. My dad's family has pastors all over Wayne and Wilson Counties. And I mean this in the *most* humble way (these are my words, not theirs), both of my families are kind of a big deal in these small towns; I try to be on my best behavior when I'm in the area.

As I said earlier, I've been going to banquets since the days of the Moose Lodge, sang at least twice when it was at the Seymour Johnson Airforce Base, sang and had words at the Dillard Building, and even at the last in person banquet at the Maxwell Center, my sister and I won a fabulous trip for 2 but never went because the pandemic started a few months later. ☹ One of the first times I was asked to sing at a Norwayne Alumni program was in 1997 by my Aunt Cappi, which you may know as the late, great Catherine Fleming Uzzell. If she asked me, I was going to make it happen. Alumni weekend was a family affair and a Labor Day Weekend tradition for us. A chance for us to get dressed up, and I am my mama's child so any reason to get "fancy" was fine with me! Sparkly outfits? Say less! Mama 'nem would stay in the lobby for the dance social but only to chat and catch up with old classmates because they didn't dance, while I was busy trying to get a glimpse of the "friends" of the "Alumni & Friends" showing up ready to hit the floor. I would be enthralled by the old school jams and thinking "Y'ALL STILL GOT IT!"

I attended faithfully until I moved to Atlanta in 2002 but would come back for my parents, aunts and uncles honored years. I hadn't planned on coming in 2011, but word on the street was that an anonymous donor had paid for Aunt Cappi's Lifetime Membership, as she was battling pancreatic cancer. I bought a plane ticket that week, packed a cocktail dress and was at the banquet that night. They presented her with the Lifetime Membership; she mustered up the strength in her weak state and gave a thank you speech that encouraged us and sent a Holy Ghost fit through the banquet hall just as if she had finished singing. The annual gospel concert was the next day. This would be the first time the Fleming Sisters would be a featured guest without the musician and leader of most of the songs. Aunt Cappi asked me and some of my cousins who were there to help the sisters sing and play for the event. With lumps in our throats, we agreed. We knew we had to do it for her, for her sisters, grandma and for the community to let them know her legacy would go on regardless, all for the Glory of God as always. She had two requests, one of which for us to dust off an oldie but goodie they never recorded but she wrote it for another group, and they wanted me to lead "Tell It." Can you say pressure??? I mean God used us, we did SANG, but understand IT WAS ALL GOD and we all were a wreck when we finished. I stood at her bedside that night, gave her a kiss on the forehead and she responded "Aww, sweetnin!" the loving moniker she called her nieces. That weekend would be the last public appearance our beautiful, loving, local celebrity would ever make and that night would be the last time I would see her. I flew back to Atlanta getting calls and updates. While we are a family of strong faith, and prayers for her healing were going up all over the land, her prognosis needed a miracle. Viola Catherine Fleming Uzzell left us a little over a month later. My faith was *shook* and I thought to myself "Ok, God, this needs a biblical, burning bush, wet fleece, explanation" because I felt if God was going to heal anyone it was going to be her. Literally, even at her service, in a fit of grief, I felt like maybe with my faith I will touch her and pick her up, we'll go out like "Weekend at Bernie's." *shrug* (Yes, that really happened and in retrospect I chuckle because I can imagine Aunt Cappi looking down like "Really?") My family is strong but still we were in shambles with a heartbreak no one was sure how to navigate.

(Now, I'm sure you're thinking by now "Ummm, the first word of the title is JOY, but this has made me a little sad." Oh, but don't worry, I'm getting to that. Just keep reading and I promise there's something that is almost sure to make you laugh in the end, but you need to understand the journey to be encouraged.)

I flew back to Atlanta with tears in my eyes. I worked in higher education and residence life but some of my students really, really enjoyed being away from their parents which created lots of school paperwork for dismissals, incident/police reports, many long nights and me looking over my shoulder. In all these years this was the first time I wasn't eager to get back to Atlanta. We were all close to Aunt Cappi but it was no secret my mother had lost her sister and best friend. Not to mention, we had been hit with several other close deaths of family (including Aunt Ruth, another Norwayne Alum) and friends that year. It was a rough year all around and I could hear the proverbial straw causing the camel a herniated disc at the very least. My doctor took me out of work for 2 weeks to rest and with the holiday season approaching, I was prescribed antidepressants and unashamedly took them. (Mental health matters!) I returned to work on a Thursday. My student staff (my good babies) surprised me with a birthday cake that Friday, which I shared with everyone in the office. On that Sunday, I turned thirty-five and kept it low-key but was grateful. I went to work the next day and as usual, my coworker and I were called to a student concern just before lunch. We decided we'd type the report after coming back from lunch. When we returned, my boss peeped over my cubicle and said "Hey, can I talk to you for a second", I said "Sure", and as we were walking towards his office I heard my coworker say "What is happening?!" but again, there was always SOMETHING happening!!! I never thought "for a second" this would lead to me being let go. I returned to my desk to get personal items, emotionless and in shock. I realized my co-worker's loud exclamation was because when I went down the hall, someone immediately came from around the other side to get my computer. It was sudden and unceremonious. There were no goodbyes. And since I worked in housing, I stayed on site. I had a month to pack, leave my place and leave Atlanta if I didn't find another job. I was depressed, but somehow relieved, yet still felt like a failure. I was the worship leader at my church, I had great friends there, I was doing pretty good for myself… I mean I was about to buy my dream car for my birthday but they didn't have the color I wanted when I went that Saturday. (God knows, don't He?!) I came home twice in November like normal but only my immediate family knew I was coming back to live with my parents after Thanksgiving. I didn't want to add my bad news to what was already going to be a rough holiday season for our family. Early December, I drove back home with tears running down my face the entire four-and half-hour ride. Mom hugged me tight, daddy offered to get my things out of the car but I told him to wait because I just couldn't do it. I got in bed that night exhausted and that's where I stayed for days on end. I would come out to eat so they wouldn't be too worried. If it weren't for the pictures, I wouldn't have much of a memory of the holiday. I kept thinking "I just need to make it through Christmas then I'll look for work and move back to Atlanta." That was MY plan, but I'm pretty sure God laughed at those plans as He knew what He was doing was eventually going to work for the good…

Since I was back in North Carolina, I wasn't in a rush to leave grandma's house after Christmas Day like years past. I wore old sweats, no makeup, hair pulled back and ate all the goodies my aunts cooked to spoil us. Occasionally I cried because missing Aunt Cappi

52

and Aunt Ruth were still very fresh but laughed because the house was still full of love and merriment. Now understand, BOTH of my grandma's are my whole heart so when it comes to them, I'm just as giddy to be at their homes as an adult as I was as a child. And this particular time was no different. I was sitting at the table bothering Grandma Ida and acting like I was going to be her unofficial nurse assistant. Although we had an automatic one, I picked up the real sphygmomanometer (the technical term for blood pressure cuff) and had my actual nurse-cousin teach me how to use it. Again, thinking nothing of it, just being silly with my Ida B, but all things still work together for the good, right? I checked her blood sugar/blood pressure and joked she couldn't have any more desserts or tea. We chuckled as usual, I stayed for dinner and decided to leave the next morning. We had made it through Christmas without incident… almost.

I got dressed to leave that next morning and heard a commotion. Grandma woke up and wasn't feeling well. My aunt had checked her blood sugar and when I walked in the room, she didn't look like the chuckling, jolly, lady I loved to tease. I went into crisis mode. This was my chance to put the knowledge of checking blood pressure I randomly learned the day before to use. We called 911. The paramedics came, said she needed to go get checked out and we ended up taking grandma to the hospital ourselves. When we arrived, we were met at the ER by my aunt and cousin (both nurses) but when they opened the door to get her out of the truck she was showing signs of a stroke. 2 days after Christmas, a little more than two months after her daughter's passing and about 9 months after her own sister's sudden passing. I stood there numb and silent, staring at her twisted face, but screaming "DEAR GOD, NO!" on the inside. I started sending messages to let my other cousins know the details and to pray. Again, although we were a strong family, I knew we were not ok, well, at least I wasn't.

They kept grandma for a day or so and released her but she needed someone to stay with her. And who had all the free time in the world to stay with my Ida B and be a few miles away from my Georgia Lee so I could visit her more too? That's right… the recently unemployed granddaughter who was back in North Carolina. Talk about a "homecoming." I moved from one of the most happening cities in the country to spending my weeks in a one stop light, rural town that only had one place to get a decent cup of coffee. Sheesh! I could spend my time looking for work online, while helping grandma and taking her to appointments. Didn't I tell y'all God knows and all things work for the good that love the Lord? (That's Bible, ROMANS 8:28!) My life was in a state of uncertainty, but one thing was certain, even at my lowest and in my disappointment, I loved the Lord and so did my praying grandma.

Part 2: An Unexpected Homecoming: The Joy Found in the Journey

I ended up spending quite a bit of time with Grandma Ida during her months of recovery. We had some fun, we butted heads and we really got to know each other as adults. We shared our commentary on TV shows (oh we loved Scandal once I explained it was a "story" and Obama was still the president at the time) We learned how to SKYPE. She told me stories of her late husband, my grandpa Doug, with a twinkle still in her eye (and this may be why I'm still single because no one has kept that twinkle in my eye for more than a few months, but hey *shrugs*) She even learned to appreciate most of my cooking except when I agreed to try to clean and fry fresh fish. That happened once; I butchered the fish and it ended up being fish nuggets. We went to Mayflower if we had a taste for seafood after that. But the trips to Mayflower or anywhere with her were always an adventure. That time in the small town and my boredom from being in bed at 10pm like her, led me to start a blog to get my racing thoughts out of my head. I called it "My Life, Your Laugh." The following stories of me and Ida B are 100% true and were originally published there. I still laugh at these and I'm sure you will too.

Can she hear me now??? (September 2012)

One of the joys of being unemployed and moving back to NC is I get to spend more time with my 83yr old grandma who's lived in the same small town she was born in all of her life. (I've mentioned her a few times on my blog before) She thinks I'm wild and I think the same about her, so when we get together it's all the way LIVE! Her wisdom is invaluable and she's very sharp with her quick-witted comebacks. She's in decent health and is still in her right mind, but she is very amazed with the technological advances and innovations she's seen happen in her lifetime. She's had cable tv for a while, has a cell phone, wi-fi (my aunt got it hooked up at the house), but Grandma is still in awe whenever she gets on Skype with her grandkids, great-grand kids, and great-great grandkids who live several states away. The first time she skyped she went on for days about how they always said one day you'd be able to see and talk to somebody, but she still can't believe she could see them on "the tv" (computer screen). I can only imagine how someone who was born during the depression and remembers when TVs were invented feels when they see today's technology. I mean even I think we're but a few years away from flying cars like the Jetsons and I'm a generation X-er. But nothing prepared me for the episode that took place while we were on vacation...

I was invited to tag along on vacation to Virginia Beach with my youngest aunt and my grandma. I figured since I wasn't working yet I might as well enjoy the liberty to travel once again. So we left Wednesday and typed in our destination to my aunt's built-in GPS, but at the advice of several relatives we decided not to go the suggest route and take some quicker back roads. After what seemed like driving all day (but it was only about an hour and half) on these two lane country roads we end up in civilization and decide to use the GPS to the rest of the way. Not only did it get us to our hotel, but we used it throughout the city to get us around. Grandma was very quiet and listened intently to the directions from the female voice and referred to it as "she", "her" or "the lady". Often, she asked "What did she say?" making sure my aunt turned and followed "her" directions.

On our second day of vacation, we decided to find a mall and once again "the lady" got us to our destination without issue. Since it was a mall, we didn't follow the GPS to the very end of the route and my aunt began to drive around the perimeter of the mall parking lot so we could scope out the anchor stores and surrounding shops near the mall. Me and my aunt begin pointing out various stores "Oooh Dillard's." "Oh, an Old Navy" and grandma says excitedly while pointing "Look... there's a MAXY'S!" We look in the direction she's pointing, and my aunt says with a chuckle "Mama... that's MACY'S" and we all began to laugh. (Grandma is known for not quite reading something right, so even when we correct her, she laughs at herself just as much as we do.)

I start laughing even harder because she's tickled herself, but then grandma stops laughing and says shamefully "Y'all better hush that fuss before them people hear you!"

My aunt looks at me, and I look at her like "who is she talking about?" I looked out the window thinking maybe there were some people in the parking lot or perhaps a car beside us. No one is near us.

So my aunt turns to her and says "Uhhh,Mama what people?"

Grandma says with all seriousness in a whispery voice..."The lady 'nem" and points to the GPS screen!!!

My aunt and I looked at each other and LOST IT! I mean I hollered even louder. My aunt is trying to explain to her there really isn't a lady talking to us but we can't pull it together. We're laughing so hard that once again grandma starts laughing which only makes me laugh even harder.

And the more I thought about how grandma referred to the GPS as "the lady" and was unusually quiet the whole trip, the funnier it was and the louder I hollered!!!

Later on that evening we finally figured out why she might have been confused a little. The GPS and Bluetooth work very similarly so when we call someone they can hear everyone in the car and we're thinking grandma must've thought "the lady" giving the directions could hear us too.

I don't know who the female voice behind the Dodge GPS systems is but wherever you are in the satellite atmosphere... Thank you for the directions and the best laugh I've had in a while!

The Amazing Wheelchair Race! (May 2014)

From the chronicles of Nilly and Ida B:

Now that my heart rate has returned to normal, I can tell the story.

Yesterday I was once again hustled by my grandma to take her shopping. Initially I was told she wanted to go to Walmart, but I knew she had more up her sleeve. Before we left the house, she told me she wants me to take her to buy MORE flowers for her yard. I put emphasis on MORE because I have taken her to Lowe's and Walmart on my last two visits to get flowers, but there is a local plant farm she wanted to go to because they also have vegetable seedlings for her two vegetable gardens as well. Before we left the house, this 86yr old woman, with arthritic knees, who has no strength in her legs and uses a rolling walker, tries to convince me not to bring her wheelchair on this shopping trip. Ummm, ma'am how do you expect to walk around to look at flowers??? She claims they have a "riding cart" that she can use to get around, but I followed my first mind and loaded the wheelchair in the car anyway. So we head out to the plant farm...

I knew I was in for a time when this old lady decides to argue with my phone GPS and the signs along the route that are pointing towards this local business. Grandma is still very sharp for her age, but she does have her "senior moments". I follow the signs and GPS and end up at what appears to be a regular house with a very large back yard, but

57

the sign says "LONGS PLANT FARM" so I knew I was in the right place, whether she believed it or not. Like most local, rural, agriculture businesses, there was a dirt path to drive on and an extension of the path for handicapped parking. Just as I thought, I saw no signs of a "riding cart" at this establishment. I saw lots of plants, abandoned greenhouses, an appliance graveyard (a la Sanford & Son), rusted red wagons to carry the plants, but nothing motorized that grandma could ride which means I was going to have to push her through the actual sand in the yard located in the actual "Sand Hills" of eastern North Carolina. I was already over this outing, but grandma has been trying to get someone to bring her to this place and it was too late to turn back now.

I knew I couldn't push her around, grab the flowers she couldn't reach, put them in the wagon and pull the wagon all at the same time, but I came up with a system. I would put the wagon in a central location in the nursery, grab the flowers, run them back and forth, then push her to the next section. Seems like a good plan, right? Well, I didn't factor in grandma's stubbornness and pride into my plan.

Picture it: The section we're browsing in is covered in black tarp on top of sand on uneven ground. I'm picking out gorgeous blooms and cayenne pepper plants as instructed, running them to my wagon in the center of a maze of flowers and greenery. Next thing I know I hear my grandma's signature high pitched voice saying, "It feels like it's going by itself". Y'all, I look up and my grandma is sliding across the tarp, rolling down a hill towards the car, holding on to her pocketbook for dear life like Sophia from "Golden Girls." I couldn't even scream. I just gasped and took off running to catch this runaway wheelchair. All I could think was how am I going to explain to everyone how the matriarch of the family ended up injured from being tossed across this plant farm and covered in sand!!! JEEEEEESUSSSS!

After I catch her, just before she drifts into the driveway, grandma is laughing while I'm trying to swallow hard because it feels like my heart is in my throat. She's chuckling and telling me she was just trying to push herself so I wouldn't have to be worried with pushing her too. Really old lady??? Really??? Now is not the time to be "Ms. Independent"!

I gave up on my system and pushed her a few feet with one hand and pulled the wagon with the other. You can best believe I didn't step more than a yard from her without putting on the brakes!!! You will not have my cousins looking at me sideways because I literally let grandma get run over by a reindeer!

2022 update: I NEVER TOOK HER TO ANOTHER PLANT NURSERY AFTER THAT AND HAVEN'T TO THIS DAY!

Part 3: An Unexpected Homecoming: The Joy Found in the Journey

I spent almost 3 years praying and hoping to move back to Atlanta, until I decided to let go and let God. Looking back on the time I spent in Wayne County was a blessing. Watching my grandma Ida get up every morning to read her Bible and pray for all four generations behind her and extended branches of our family was what I needed to see. Being able to pop in on my grandma Georgia (the oldest mother of the local church and still serving), seeing her smile, still watching The Young and the Restless with her after all these years and being to show up to her church for homecomings and to sing for Women's Day made me even more grateful. Walking the country roads for exercise, breathing in the fresh air, visiting family cemeteries to feel the connection to loved ones gone on, driving by houses/sites connected to us, but then being able to hear the stories from the past made me realize my legacy of faith in God was connected to my family and I found strength in returning to my roots. I had quoted scriptures about faith and mercy going from generation to generation, but now I was able to experience it for myself.

In 2014, 20 years after being a Norwayne Scholarship recipient, I was asked once again to participate in the Labor Day Weekend Festivities.

It was the week of the event, and I was prepared to say yes to singing as usual, but to my surprise, I was asked to give the invocation/prayer of thanks before we had dinner. I had not been able to attend in previous years, but I had just begun a great career and was able to attend. (Again, I live for a microphone and a reason to get dressed up, so say less!) It was so very fitting to be able to join in with the Norwayne Alumni & Friends to lead us in a moment of thanks. It was also that night I was able to give my first donation in honor of my 20th year out of high school and give back to the organization that first gave to me. Since then, I know the importance of supporting this great organization. The following year I rallied behind my Aunt Dot when she became Alumni Queen. I've somehow ended up in the parade trucks with the family. I even started a t-shirt line a few years ago and was asked to design the shirts for the class of 1969 50th year celebration and designed an exclusive Norwayne Alumni shirt in which all the proceeds from each shirt purchased are donated to the association. When the banquet went virtual in 2020, I helped with the presentations and one of the highlights of my 2021 was being asked to sing and emcee the annual gospel fest 10 years after my Aunt Cappi had asked me to sing at the same event before she passed. It was as if I had come full circle. There would literally be no me without the products of Norwayne Alumni & Friends. I celebrate this organization, its purpose, its impact on past, present and future generations along with all the many blessings to come. Happy 50th Homecoming Weekend Norwayne Alumni and Friends!

Oh, and I'm grown now so, while mama 'nem will be in the lobby during the dance, I can't make any promises if I hear "The Electric Slide" after the banquet this year. As the young folks say "TURN UP!"

Continuing My Story:
PEACE AND LOVE TO ALL

I am the eighth child, of thirteen, born to Noah and Annie Dobson Harvey. I am Blessed by God to be one of ten still living. There are five boys and five girls. Anyone who knows us, knows that we are a close knit family. We have each other's back, always have and always will - we love like that. My husband of 44 years passed in 2018. We have five beautiful and loving children, and seven grandchildren who are loved very much.

I came to Norwayne in the fourth grade and graduated in 1969, as a matter of fact I was the last in the family to graduate from Norwayne. My oldest brother Nathaniel was the first one; he graduated in 1961. My brother Billy and my sister Betty Joyce both graduated in 1965. My brother Billy and his friend Robert Hill tried out to be cheerleaders and made the squad. You couldn't tell those two short men anything, they cheered throughout high school. Billy, like a lot of people, married his high school sweetheart, Nevelene Sauls.

I became a member of the Alumni when it was first organized. I was the first secretary and thus far I have only missed two reunions. I guess my love for Norwayne and the Alumni prompted two of my daughters to become members. My daughter Regina has been one of the queens, and if I must say so myself, she made a Beautiful Queen.

In my life there have been tragedies, miracles, and many blessings. As the song says I have had some good days and I have had some mountains to climb but all of my good days outweigh my bad days, and I won't complain. True friends come a dime a dozen and I am blessed to say that I have friends from the first grade. Coming up in a large family taught us how to love and appreciate so many things.

When we get together with our children and their children, oh what a time we have loving on each other.

Since Mary wrote this story, and before this book was printed, she lost her brother, Bobby Harvey, Charles B. Aycock, Class of 1971. That leaves her with four brothers now.

Willie Mae Harvey' Shehee
Charles B. Aycock   Class of 1974

A Snapshot of My Life

"Run, Run, Run! He's coming, Run!!"

Those words were yelled soon after I started the first grade at
Pikeville Training School. I had no idea why a voice was yelling for
us to run, nor did I know who we were supposed to be running from
and then, I saw a real live monster. He was chasing this little girl and
he looked awful. I'm sure you think that I am exaggerating about
seeing a monster; however, to a five-year-old girl this boy looked like
a monster. He had turned his eyelids up and you could see the red
blood vessels on the under lids of his eyes and this made him look
like something from your nightmares. I later found out that the
monster boy's name was Carl and he decided that I was someone he
did not want to scare. He started treating me like a little sister and no
one was allowed to bother me.

My name is Willie Mae Harvey' Shehee and I am the tenth child of
thirteen children. When I accepted this writing assignment, I was 64
years old. Being that old gives me lots of things I could write about so
I decided to give you just a glimpse into my life and hopefully it will
help you understand if only just a little about the person I am today.
For example, I am the only child of my parents who was born on a
Sunday. Our Mother told me that I came in time for Sunday school
but not in time for her to be there. It's a good thing that Sunday's
child is full of Grace because I was a very colicky baby who cried a
lot, so I have been told. Hopefully, that has changed, and my loudness
is now from joy instead of pain.

You would think that since I was one of thirteen, I would at least ride
the same school bus as one of my siblings, right? Wrong! I was on the
bus alone. I remember the first time another rider asked me who was
the White man standing with me as I waited for the bus. I was so

confused. What White man, I asked. Are you talking about my dad? I was told that he couldn't be my dad because he was White. My father was a light skinned Black man and although he farmed, he didn't turn brown instead he turned a reddish bronze color. I was teased so much until I asked Mom to ask him not to stand with me. Unbeknownst to me he still stood beside the house to make sure I got on the bus safely. That's what parents do, protect us even when we don't realize it.

I am now at Norwayne School, and this is where I always wanted to be. All my older siblings went to this school. Some of you who are reading this will remember Hiawatha and how he would turn Norwayne School out. Here I am once again at a school where other students are yelling for you to run. He was a nice guy most of the time and I never had any problems with him, but he sure knew how to turn the school out when he was having one of his epileptic fits. Norwayne School was integrated while I attended classes there. It was a very sad and trying time for all of us who loved Norwayne.

My high school years were at Charles B. Aycock High School. When I first started school there, I did not feel welcome. I soon decided that since I had to go there, I would make the best of it, and I would be comfortable there. We had to overcome lots of stereotypes and prejudices from our White classmates. Some of them just like some of us had never had a friend from a different race. I embraced it and made good friends from both races. I eventually decided to try out for the cheerleading squad and became President of the cheerleaders in our division. After much debate we finally convinced the school to allow us to celebrate Black History Day, yes back then it was just one day. We had no idea how many White parents would be against that and would withdraw their children from school. Death threats were made, and the State Troopers had to make sure that we entered the school safely on Monday after death threats were made over the weekend. We had White students whose parents let them go to school but were not supposed to stay in the gym for the Black History celebration, so they walked out. That was a very sad day for us and our school. Things eventually calmed down and we started to look forward to prom and our graduation.

Three months before our high school graduation in 1974 one of our White classmates was drinking and driving with an underclassman in his truck when he ran into my parents' car almost killing them both. Sadly, the young man riding with him lost his life. Three months after the car wreck and one week after our graduation and a couple of days before my sister would be coming to get me for a summer job where she worked, our family suffered another life altering event. My oldest brother and second oldest sister were killed by my sisters' estranged husband. That is something you never recover from; but life goes on.

Several years have passed since the three months in 1974 that changed our family forever and I met James, the man I would marry. It is amazing that James and I met because he was in the military, and I didn't date military guys unless I knew them before they joined the service. I had two friends from work who didn't think the same way and it didn't matter that one was Black and the other was White. They both decided that they had met the perfect man for me. He supervised the guys they were dating so they felt this would be wonderful. They each kept insisting I meet this guy for months and I always refused. One night I went to a club with the Black friend, and he was there. Yes, the same guy I had been refusing to meet for almost a year was at the same club I was and at the same time, kismet! Before he could come where we were; just like in the movies, our eyes met from across the room and our future was sealed. We would be together and coming from different worlds, I knew it would not be easy. I am totally a Mommas' girl and never wanted to leave her nor the rest of our family, but I would have to if I wanted to be with him. By this time James was stationed in Delaware and we would travel to meet one another. We were married after dating for two years and before our first anniversary I was pregnant with our only child.

Our first assignment as a military couple was in Minot, North Dakota. The saying was "why not Minot"! I soon found out it was because of the extreme cold weather. Our son was four months old when we moved there and I was terrified to be going somewhere without my family there to help raise our child. I didn't know how I was going to do it. We next moved to Albuquerque, New Mexico and I loved it there. The weather did not get into the minus degrees like North Dakota and my family could visit. In New Mexico I became friends with native Americans from tribes I never knew about. I also became friends with Latinos and Hispanics. Coming from our part of Eastern North Carolina, I was beginning to see the big wide world.

We lived in Albuquerque for many years and left there to go to Illinois. In Albuquerque, we found a community of people who were tolerant of each person's diverse backgrounds and bonded over those differences. In Belleville, Illinois we found nice people, but we also found people who were more prejudiced than I knew from growing up in North Carolina. During this time some of the little communities around us still adhered to the sundowner laws. That meant that if you were Black, you should never let the sun go down on you while in those communities. The city of Belleville at this time had been around for about two hundred years and had never employed a person of color. Oprah Winfrey was going strong with her talk show at this time and decided to pay our city a visit. Just before Oprah came, the city of Belleville hired its first Black city employee. He was the city janitor. When Oprah asked the mayor about the first Black city employee being the city janitor the mayor said that his nephew had applied for that position and if it was good enough for his nephew it was good enough for a Black person. Living in Illinois we were confronted with deep seated prejudice everywhere we turned. At our sons' grade school, I had to threaten to be in his classroom everyday if that was going to be the only way he would be treated fairly. I also found that sometimes our people hurt themselves by staying complacent and being afraid of change.

Belleville was also the city, or more importantly, Scott Air Force Base where I would find myself fighting for my life. I became seriously ill while living there and surely goodness and mercy was following me and prayers were protecting me. Due to my illness, I had an extremely high temperature which caused my team of doctors to pack bags of ice around my head and had an industrial type of fan blowing on me to prevent me from having brain damage. Some might say it worked and some might wonder. At this base hospital at this particular time, they had a pay phone that could be pushed from room to room, this obviously was before cell phones were everywhere.

The nurse who was in charge on the day shift told me that in the first four days that I was admitted, she believed there had been about three hundred calls requesting information about me. She asked me if I had a large family and exactly how many were in the medical field. If I hadn't been feeling so bad, I would have thought it funny. My fever was so high I was given fluids to combat that, and I will admit I looked like the Pillsbury Doughboy's sister. The night that my fever would finally break; unbeknownst to me, my mom had asked the members of Hooks Grove Missionary Baptist Church in Pikeville, North Carolina to pray for me. I had asked her not to come until I was close to being released from the hospital because I knew I would need her once I went home. On the night my fever finally broke I had never felt so hot in my life. I was able to get off my bed and lie on the floor. I needed as much of my body to touch something. anything as cold as possible and as fast as possible anything at all would do.

As I was lying there the night nurse came in and saw me on the floor and starts calling for help. He thought that I had fallen off the bed. I tried telling him that I'm going to be alright because I could see prayers going up to heaven on my behalf. This made him think that I was hallucinating and he became more desperate to get me some help. Suddenly, I heard a woman's voice say, "she's going to be alright." She said she sees prayers going up to heaven on her behalf. I would later learn that she was a preacher's wife and she said, "you must have some powerful praying people in your life." She told me that she had never heard of anyone who saw the prayers going up for them before. I had a long recovery, but those prayers changed everything for me.

Our next assignment as a family was in Okinawa, Japan. I absolutely loved living there with one exception. It was too far from our families and from Los Angeles it was a very long seventeen-hour flight. I kept trying not to think about all the time spent flying over the ocean. While living there we went to South Korea and the ladies will appreciate the amount of shopping you can do in Korea. One day as I walked into the break room at work, I heard a Japanese woman say Naomi Campbell so I turned around so I could see Naomi Campbell myself not realizing she was speaking about me. It was then I realized that this woman didn't know what Naomi Campbell looked like because I didn't have one feature that looked like her other than we were both Black.

While living on the Island of Okinawa which is about seventy miles long and about seven miles wide, we were told to keep some local money in the car because some of the roads are toll roads and if you keep driving you would eventually end up back where you started or on one of the toll roads. My boss had once been stationed at Ft. Bragg in Fayetteville and knew about our great eastern North Carolina vinegar-based barbeque sauce. When my boss found out that I was from North Carolina he told me that if I could get someone in my family to send some barbeque sauce, he would buy a pig and we would make barbeque for all the employees. Oh yes, I had my family send a case of Scotts barbeque sauce and we had a good time. I also had my family send me some red candy apple mix. I made candy apples and my Okinawan co-workers were excited and did not believe anything so beautiful could be eaten and wanted to save them. I had to convince them to eat them because we know the candy will melt.

While on Okinawa I met friends from the top four branches of the military. This is significant because the branches don't usually hang around each other unless in a military role. My husband was in the Air Force, we lived on a Naval Base and I worked on a Marine Camp. I ate my first seaweed, sushi and squid while living there. I was lucky because of my size I was able to shop for clothes out in the local community and not always on the base. They even had yen stores which are the equivalent of our dollar stores, and the pastries were so good I would love to go back on that long flight just for some. Living there I also had friends from Thailand, The Philippines, Okinawa, Japan, Cambodia, Hawaii just to name a few and found that we are more alike than we commonly think. I should tell you that the Okinawans are not regular Japanese. The Japanese conquered them and they became Japanese citizens. I learned different customs and traditions from these wonderful people that I still cherish today.

We have also lived in Washington, DC, Maryland, Virginia, and Georgia. There is so much I could write about the places where we lived and the people I met; but I truly just wanted to give you a snapshot of my life and to say that the love of family was instilled in us from the time we were born, and it is still so very important. For me family isn't just the people who were born in the same house or same family as you were. In my world family also means all the people who you love and care about as if they were family.

I hope you enjoyed reading this snapshot of my life and in the words of my favorite song as sung by Louis Armstrong *"I see skies of blue and clouds of white, The blessed day, the dark sacred night. And I think to myself what a wonderful world."*

Bobby Gene Holmes   *Norwayne Class of 1964*

Glory to God and My Village

My Story began on April 16, 1945, when I was born to the late William C. Holmes and Louvenia Holmes in Wayne County, North Carolina. I attended Eureka Elementary School until the county decided to build a school that would include first through twelfth grades. That is when Norwayne School was established.
I was struggling to maintain good grades because I worked three days a week and attended school only two days a week. This was very discouraging! My eighth-grade teacher failed me in my first year at Norwayne. That was so embarrassing, but it motivated me to do my best.

When I was in ninth grade, Mr. Montague, the Basketball Coach, saw how tall I was and encouraged me to join the Basketball team. This was one of the best things that ever happened to me. It also motivated me to stay in school and keep my grades up. It was such an honor and a privilege for two years to play on the Varsity Basketball team, that we did not lose a home game in those two years. We also played in the State Championship at AT&T College Greensboro, North Carolina

I received an athletic scholarship to Fayetteville State College in Fayetteville, North Carolina. Unfortunately, I was unable to attend therefore I decided to seek work in Washington, DC. Since I did not attend college, this proved to be one of the best decisions for me. I was blessed to gain employment at the U. S. Government Printing Office, where I became a Pressman. I was trained as an Apprentice, Pressman, and Supervisor, and it was funded by the U. S. Government. I was employed at the Government Printing Office for 29 years and nine months.

I was blessed to marry the love of my life, Dorothy Best. We have been married for fifty-two years. From this union two children were born, Derrick M. Holmes and Stephanie Holmes-Turner. We also have a daughter-in-law Egypt Holmes, a son-in-law Lenwood Turner, and seven grandchildren.

70

I retired from the U. S. Government Printing Office to Pastor Deliverance Church of Christ, located in Capitol Heights, MD. It has been a joy to serve the people of God. In 2016, I was consecrated as Bishop of the Deliverance Church of Christ Association.

I give all the glory to God for His wisdom; to my parents' guidance, corrections, my pastors, and my church leaders for my spiritual development. Also, I thank the educators of Norwayne High School for how they instructed and motivated me to pursue higher education.

Ann Hunt Jones Smith   Norwayne Music Teacher

Unforgettable Memories

From my toddler years through college days, I had heard about Jesus, and thought I knew Him. Surrounded by godly parents, older women, teachers and ministers, the Name Jesus was often mentioned. However, it was September 1964, in a sunrise Worship Service when I encountered an unforgettable experience. The parable in Matthew 25 convicted me as I heard the story of the wise and foolish virgins. I realized that I was not ready for the return of the Bridegroom. Tears flowed from my eyes as I pondered over my lost condition. Surely, my living was in vain.

Suddenly, a tunnel appeared before me. An extended hand emerging through a stream of bright light drew me to want to reach out and grasp the hand. My fingertips were close to the outreached hand; my whole body seemed to be afire. Gushes of praise and thanksgiving erupted from the depths of my soul. Heartfelt cries for forgiveness were uttered as the sins I had ignorantly, yet willfully committed flashed through my mind. I cannot remember now, nor did I know then, how I moved from standing in front of a pew in the center aisle to the open door in the rear of this tabernacle. I only remember that my head seemed to have been lifted from my body. A supernatural change - a transformation in my overall being had occurred. Here, in that early morning service, I believed that Jesus touched me. It was here in Wayne County, North Carolina that my journey to follow Jesus became foremost in my life.

In 1958, I had completed college and eagerly anticipated teaching music in my hometown, Raleigh, North Carolina. The one vacancy for a music teacher was in Wake County located in a rural community about twelve miles west of Raleigh. My assignment as music teacher included my teaching Civics, English, Health Education. My lunch hour was used to rehearse the chorus I had organized from the one music class. My evenings at home were spent studying to keep ahead of the students in the subjects I had to teach besides music. It was a stressful situation. I had been trained to be a music teacher from grades one through twelve.

December 1959, at twenty-two years old I married. My husband who was in the Air Force had a two week leave, then he had to return to his base in California. In February I learned that I had conceived a child "on my honeymoon." That very same day my joy turned to sorrow. My father had to be rushed through snow-covered streets to Saint Agnes Hospital where he was pronounced "dead on arrival."

Added to being a new wife came the role of being a new mother. I was so grateful for my mother's help and support as I adjusted to my new responsibilities. After being at home with my baby for one year, I focused on continuing my teaching career. There were no positions available in Wake County, but I was made aware of two openings in Wayne County. How could I travel fifty-eight miles to and from a job? My greatest concern was being away from my baby. I would have to live in a community near the school. After much discussion with my husband and my mother, with whom we lived, I was convinced to arrange for an interview with a J. H. Carney, Principal of a Norwayne School in Fremont, North Carolina.

I do not remember who drove me to Goldsboro, North Carolina and out to the Wayne County school. My interview with Mr. Carney was very thorough. He even walked me to the Norwayne Gym that housed the piano and asked me to play it. I could see that Mr. Carney was very impressed by my performance. In a few weeks I was notified that I had been selected from two other applicants. After completing an application with Wayne County School System and signing a contract with Mr. Carney, it was very necessary to locate housing and to secure transportation for the weeks school was in session. Mr. Carney helped me in both instances.

Being away from my husband five days per week placed a strain on our relationship. Daily I functioned in a state of bewilderment; especially, at the end of the day living in a rented room. The first year at Norwayne was very productive. However, when I returned for a second school term, I was twenty-four years old and three months pregnant with a second child. Besides coping with morning sickness, I was extremely tired. How did I make it from September to December? Mr. Carney was furious when I told him I would have to take maternity leave. Somehow, I had managed to camouflage my pregnancy. He spoke emphatically: "You can go home and have that baby, but I want you back here for my commencement music." When the baby was born in March, another teacher was taking maternity leave. I returned to her position as an English teacher with a period set aside for teaching chorus. Having had to teach English at my first job in 1958, I was more prepared to fulfill this teaching assignment for two months at Norwayne school.

One of my greatest challenges was to teach and discipline my students without giving into the anger I was withholding. My marriage was falling apart. I had evidence of infidelity on my husband's part; I was also being tempted to engage in an illicit affair. One day, in desperation, I hopped on the school bus and rode home with students. I even spent the night. (Of course, Mr. Carney did not get wind of this.). It was the prayers of Sister Sampson and Sister Pitt, parents of my students, that fortified me to have courage to move through legal separation, rent a duplex apartment for me and my girls, and find someone in the neighborhood to care for my girls during the school days.

Not only were my Norwayne students very talented and eager to learn, but they were loving and compassionate. Somehow, they seemed to be aware of my circumstances. Several parents allowed their girls to become weekend sitters for my girls. Some students even came during the week to allow me to attend nearby Wednesday night prayer meetings. When I talk to them now, my students can recall several exciting experiences they had during my five years as chorus teacher. What I remember are the faces of so many students, boys and girls, who respected me and trusted me to develop their singing voices. The Flemings, the Sherrods, the Artises, the Suttons, the Coleys, the Exums, the Yelvertons, the Fullers, the Sauls, the Harrises, the Lewises, the Cores, the Newsomes, the Reids , a "Singing Basketball Team," and pep club were in God's plan. It was necessary to shape and mold my character, develop my creative abilities, and HE used these to fulfill HIS plan. Above all else, I was drawn to seek Jesus. Adversity, trials, heartaches, anguish and disappointments altered my perception of the world. But GOD!! It was at Norwayne High School in Fremont, North Carolina where I was forced to cope with my life.

Dear Norwayne School, Oh, how we do adore you...

Cleveland Lewis   Norwayne   Class of 1967

A Glimpse of the Early Years

Foreword:
*I write this story as I ponder sad news that my 5*th *grade teacher, Mrs. Minnie Greenfield Carney, recently passed away at the ripe age of 103. In fact, it was that sad news that prompted me to put pen to paper and write about this particular day-in-the-life of Norwayne School. I also often remember my good friend, David Edwards. David passed on a few years ago, at the age of 65. This memoir is a tribute to the memory of these two important figures in my life's journey. There were so many other special friends and cherished memories of Norwayne School about which I could write, but space is limited. Anyway, they each know who they are.*

It all happened during the fall of 1959. I was just starting 5th grade at Norwayne School that year. It was the second year of Norwayne School's existence. The very idea of us having a brand new school was still fresh and exciting. We had beautiful new brick buildings, connected by covered walkways. Even though our school was located off the main beaten path, (actually it was in the sticks), we could boast that we had a better school campus than did the White kids.

You see, I had completed my first three years of grade school at Friendship School in Fremont - the site where St James Church now stands. My four oldest siblings, William, James, Henry, and Madie, all graduated from Friendship School. It was there that I developed a passion and lifelong love for learning. I credit Principal Cherry and his wonderful staff for their loving commitment and enduring patience toward us students. Those teachers were determined that we would be the best that we could be.

Having started first grade with little formal learning, each lesson taught was fascinating to me. I had a vivid imagination. I think I fell in love with my first grade teacher, Mrs. Raynor, as I'm sure all of the other little boys did. I still remember the primer from which she taught us to read. I could picture myself participating in the storybook adventures alongside Alice, Jerry, and Jip, their dog. I remember how Mrs. Raynor told us to practice and learn the vocabulary of that primary reader, an assignment that I literally took to heart. In fact, I can still recite that vocabulary today. She never told us that we could forget it after the first grade.

Anyway, as fate would have it, a major portion of Friendship School was completely destroyed by what may have been the worst fire ever in the history of Fremont. That incident happened during the school year, 1957-1958. Fortunately, that fire started in the evening, after the school day ended. The main building was an old dilapidated wooden structure that probably should have been condemned many years before. I believe that building was where most of the classrooms were located. Anyway, it was completely reduced to ashes in a matter of minutes.

With pot-bellied stoves as the heat source, that building was a smoldering inferno waiting to erupt. By the grace of God, no lives were lost in that horrific fire. From our house two miles away, we could clearly see the billowing smoke. Our dad drove us over to witness what turned out to be the end of an important era in local Black history. Practically all of the living Black folk in Fremont had attended school there. Anyway, we arrived just in time to witness the iconic school bell falling from the belfry. All who were there can likely still remember that haunting death knell we heard tolling as that historical symbol came crashing to the ground.

As tragic as it was, that fire incident turned out to be quite fortuitous for the local Black community. Had it not happened, we likely would not have gotten a brand new school, built exclusively for us. It was ready just in time to begin the 1958-1959 school year. Complete with a gymnasium and cafeteria. Wow! Would wonders never cease? Friendship School never had those kinds of luxuries. Prior to that time, we rarely, if ever, got any new text books or supplies. Probably never had we received a new school bus. And now, a brand new school!

Fast forward to 1959 and the fond memory about which I choose to write. As I mentioned, it was my second year at Norwayne School. Mrs. Carney was my homeroom teacher that year. As I recall, Mrs. Carney decided that our class would set up a freshwater aquarium in the classroom. As part of the learning, she decided to let us students help to complete the project.

Now, I don't know how much Mrs. Carney knew about 10 year old boys at the time, but she made the mistake of asking for two volunteers to go down to the local creek and catch some minnows (or tadpoles), I don't remember which. Anyway, out of the group of boys, all of whom likely raised their hands, she picked David Edwards and me. Big mistake!

You must understand that those days represented a more innocent time, in some respects. Yet, we were constantly reminded that Jim Crow was still the law of the land. You'd have to be there to fully appreciate the complexity of racial relationships that existed in those days. It was a time when most young boys were used to going on adventure trips, hunting, and building forts in the woods. We often hung out all day without anyone worrying. Many was the day that my younger brother Leroy and I went on such adventures carrying homemade bows and arrows, slingshots, and fishing poles.

Anyway, back to the story. There was a small creek that flowed through the woods and across the road just east of the Norwayne School campus. While Mrs. Carney must have expected David and me to go down, catch some minnows, and be back within 15 minutes, we saw this as permission for an unsupervised field trip with no particular time limit. We were determined to catch any critter we found swimming in that snake infested creek, no matter what it called itself, or how long it took to catch. I'm guessing, it must have been 30 or 40 minutes later, maybe an hour later, when Mrs. Carney sent two other boys down to see if we had drowned, and to bring us back if we hadn't. In retrospect, I regret the worry and anxiety that we must have caused her. But, boy, was that a fun day at school!

While I don't remember what, if anything, we actually caught, that adventure trip marked the beginning of a long friendship with my buddy, David. That close friendship lasted throughout our remaining years at Norwayne School. David was an only child, so perhaps in some small way, I represented the brother that he never had. Whereas I, on the other hand, was the seventh child in a family of six boys and three girls. I guess I was fascinated by David because I had never seen a kid come to school with a clean neatly pressed shirt every day. If any Lewis boy left home clean, we never made it all the way to school that way. I best remember David wearing a wide mischievous-looking grin. And, he seemingly always had his mouth chock-full of purple bubble gum, which he bought from a certain school staff member, whose name I won't mention. David managed to hold on to that winsome personality until we parted ways at graduation.

Since I mentioned earlier that our four oldest siblings were Friendship School products, I must now mention that our next four Lewis siblings, Alvester, Dorothy, Cleveland, and Leroy, all had the broader experience of attending both schools. We each started at Friendship School and completed our studies at Norwayne School. Our youngest sibling, Ollie Grey, completed eight grades at Norwayne School, then moved on to graduate from Charles B. Aycock High School.

Gary Newsome, Jr.

Norwayne Alumni Scholarship Recipient

From Struggle to Victory

A Young Man's Journey through School with a Physical Disability

I was born with cerebral palsy and school was never really easy for me. I was often viewed as different from everyone else. Teachers told me I would not succeed, that I would barely graduate high school, and not go to college. In fact, when I started preschool, the teachers and administrators tried to put me in special education classrooms. Their attempts were based on my physical disability; they didn't even consider that I could have the cognitive abilities to function in a regular classroom. My parents didn't back down, however. They made sure I was able to prove myself before allowing my arbitrary placement in special education.

Once I was placed in the traditional classroom, most of my teachers and classmates respected me. Occasionally, a student would bully me for the way I walked or the way I looked. But it was in middle school when things started to take a turn for the worse. My family had just moved to a new town, and I didn't know anybody yet. I became very withdrawn compared to my earlier years. I didn't talk to anyone and struggled to ask for help. To make matters worse, not all of my teachers believed in me. One math teacher, who specialized in teaching disabled students, told me in front of all my teachers and administrators that I would not graduate with a standard high school diploma. Instead, she said, I would get either a special diploma or a GED. My mom put that teacher in her place right then and there, but that event left its mark on me. For years, I had trouble figuring out who I wanted to be and what I wanted to do. Sometimes I even questioned if I was intelligent enough to attend college one day.

However, my parents and close friends kept encouraging me through the years that it was possible.

High school was much the same. I only had one person I considered to be a true friend during that time. I initiated conversation with as few people as possible because of how I was treated in the past. I graduated high school in 2015 and went on to earn an associate's degree from Midlands Technical College. I transferred to Winthrop University in 2018. Even before transferring to Winthrop, I still had doubts about my abilities. I wasn't certain about which major to pursue. I finally went with my gut feeling, choosing to do what I love: writing, photography, and videography. I earned my bachelor's degree in mass communication this year.

My experience at Winthrop was vastly different from all my other school experiences. The transition was hard but worth it in the end. I feel I came into my own as a person and that my work at Winthrop was valued by my fellow students, instructors and myself. All my professors believed in me and pushed me to do the best I could. I made some of the best friends I've ever had. I was accepted for who I was.

After all the hard work, I am glad to be working with Empowered to Win. I tell program participants that people will try to bring them down. I encourage them to not give up, but instead show the world what they're capable of and prove they're more than what people see on the surface. When you keep pushing, you open up possibilities that will take you further in life than you could have ever imagined.

Gary Newsome Jr. was born in Oklahoma in 1996 and works as a media specialist for Empowered to Win.

Isabella Reid   *Charles B. Aycock Class of 1972*

My Life's Canvas: "An Invitation"

I am the youngest of eleven siblings. *Remember 1972.* I will explain later. Okay, where do I begin? I'll start in my early years as a child. You see we didn't have much, I guess you can say we were poor, but we were happy.

When I was only 16 months old my dad was killed, or should I say he was murdered. The story that was told to me by my mother was that he accidentally shot himself. But when they saw Daddy, he was leaning forward. According to Daddy's death certificate there was a gunshot wound to his neck and head.

It was an unknown White man that found Daddy. This man came up to the house and told my mother that "someone needs to go check on Jack; he has shot himself." Who was this White man and how did he know my dad's name? And what was this unknown man doing that close to the house?

In the summer of 1954 Daddy had gone into town to buy some necessary items such as sugar, salt, pepper, flour, etc. Y'all know what I'm talking…because everything else was raised on the farm where Daddy helped sharecrop. On this particular day, our landlord happened to walk by, and he saw a group of White men in an alleyway with Daddy pinned up against a wall with "his hands up." Their shotguns were pointed at him. He asked them what they were doing. They replied, "This is the N***** that stole from us, and we are going to kill him." Our landlord said, "That's not the man you're looking for. That's Jack Reid; he works on my farm for me." So, they let him go.

Four months later Daddy was dead. Back in those days you didn't dare question what a White person said, no matter how tragic the situation was. If you did, the same thing was going to happen to someone else.

After Daddy's funeral, my older brother, Jack Reid, Jr. wanted to go into the military. When he went to enlist, they asked for his name, and he told them. The recruiter asked him, "Ain't you Jack Reid's boy?" He replied, "Yes sir." The recruiter then told him to go home and take care of his mother and siblings. *Now why do you think he would say that to him???* I can think of a few reasons myself:

1. Were some of them involved in my dad's murder?
2. Was the recruiter involved in some way?
3. They knew who murdered my dad?

All these questions remain unanswered to this day! I don't know if any of these men are living today, but *someone* knows what really happened to my daddy.

I can remember walking to my grandma's house, my dad's mom. That was a place I thought we would be welcome, only to find out we weren't. She could see us coming before we got there. *Not to know that* she had been talking about us.

Some of Grandma's other grandchildren heard her say, and I quote, "Here come Fannie and all those children, looking like PHARAOH'S ARMY." That's when the snickering would start. When we arrived at Grandma's house, we were always greeted with a big deceptive smile, and she'd say to us, "Hey, y'all come on in." I was named after her by the way. And this is one of the reasons why I dislike my name so much!!

And to add insult to injury, we are still being called "PHARAOH'S ARMY" by some of our relatives today and being snickered at also. UNTIL, I had had enough!! So, I let them know how we were feeling with all the name calling, the snickering, and that all the laughs they had on us weren't funny anymore and it needed to STOP before someone's feelings got hurt other than ours. At that point it didn't matter with me anymore!!!

Fast forward to 1967, I was in the eighth grade in Mr. Bryant's class when integration was beginning to happen. I remember him asking the class to section off into groups as to what school we lived nearest to Norwayne or Charles B. Aycock. I didn't know why he wanted us to do that???!!! So, I told the truth and I stood in the Charles B. Aycock group.

Over the summer we received a letter in the mail about who would be chosen or, should I say drafted, to attend Charles B. Aycock. It was between me or my sister Fannie. Lo and behold, it was me, "Yours Truly." *I cried until there were no more tears to cry!!* I remember asking my mom to let me go to New York and live with my older sisters so I could finish school there. She said no.

That first day of school in 1967, I remember getting on that bus with *all those white people.* When they saw me, "there was total silence." That went on for a little while, I'll say about a month, then it started!!! The harassment and the name calling. Let me tell y'all something; if you have never been called a "*N******" by someone of a different race, then count your Blessings. Not only was I called a *N******, but I was also called *Spook, Darky, Coon.* Whatever got a laugh, I was called it. I was the only person of color on that bus, and yes, I was afraid, and I was terrified. Me being 14 years old, "*Yes I Was.*" I was outnumbered 45 to one so what could I do? If you could have had to walk a mile in my shoes; what would you have done?? So I contracted into my shell, "My Safe Haven", and that's where I remained for a long time.

One morning I got on the bus and there was *one* empty seat but before I could get to it, one of those *mean-spirited* boys rushed and sat in it. The group of mean-spirited boys were Wayne Crumpler (remember his name); Wayne Gurley; Pat Mooring; and Wilson??? (I can't remember his last name, but I want y'all to remember his name). So, I did the only thing left for me to do, I stood up all the way to school. Back then the buses had a metal bar opening on the end of every aisle seat, so that's what I held on to with one hand while holding my books with the other, trying hard not to bump anyone. Back then all the buses were straight drive, and the bus was constantly starting, stopping, turning, and jerking. The ride lasted about an hour. *I was so miserable.* And this happened more than once.

When I got lucky enough to get a seat; I was picked on even worse. I was on the bus one afternoon and two of those *mean* boys sat in a seat behind me and the torture started again. They would count 1-2-3 and take the back of my seat and shake it, and shake it, and shake it. When I didn't respond they would eventually stop, but not until they were satisfied with their harassment toward me. There was an old jacket on the floor of the bus that had been there for a while. Feet had been wiped on it and the bus floor had been wiped with it. On this particular afternoon that I had managed to get me a seat, all of a sudden, this jacket was thrown into the back of my head, *dirt and all.* I nicely placed it back on the floor where it came from.

A neighbor of ours…I'll call him Lee H. and I would walk home together. The bus stop was in front of another neighbor's home, I'll call her Hilda C. But there was a catch to him doing that though.... Lee H. would wait until the bus was completely out of sight so that no one would see him walking with a N*****. After the bus was out of sight Lee H. would come out of Hilda C. house and walk with me the rest of the way home. When he caught up with me, I asked him who threw that jacket. He replied, "Wayne." I asked him which Wayne and he said, "Wayne Crumpler." Remember his name because it will come up again.

One afternoon when I got off the bus, I had to walk about 100 feet along the road before I reached the path that led to home. On this particular day, someone threw a pencil out the window. I know it was **GOD** that protected me. If I had taken one more step, that pencil would have struck me somewhere on my body. But instead, it landed point down in the ground. **"BUT GOD."** After that incident happened, I went to the Assistant Principal's office the next day and told him how I was being treated on that bus. He asked me for the bus driver's name and bus number. He said he would handle it. I didn't believe him. That afternoon I had an *assigned seat* for the rest of the year.

The classroom was a different story though.... there were some teachers that were prejudiced also. One of my teachers would give us a pop-quiz, then he would tell the class to exchange papers. Again, me being the only person of color in his class, no one would exchange papers with me, so I had to correct my own paper. One day at school we had to dress out for PE. In order for us to get to the athletic field we had to pass through the boys' smoking area. So, when we came out, they started to sing a little jingle... "N-E-S-T-L-E-S, Nestles makes the very best *chocolate.*" This happened a few times until we turned the table on them, and we sang our own little jingle...
 "Z-E-S-T-A, Zesta makes the very best *crackers.*" Guess what?? We didn't hear it anymore. ☺ ☺

All this happened in the 1967-68 school year. That was the year I failed the ninth grade. I was supposed to graduate in 1971 but I didn't. I was so broken, I had withdrawn so far into my shell, "My Safe Haven," where no one could hurt me. I thought about dropping out several times, but I persevered and graduated in 1972. At least I didn't drop out like Wilson did.

When school started back in 1968-69, I wasn't on the bus by myself; there were two little Black children that rode with me. Wayne Gurley and Pat Mooring would drive to school some days, and I heard them say that Wilson??? had dropped out. So that left only Wayne Crumpler. That pack of mean-spirited boys was slowly dwindling.

After all those guys graduated in 1969, over the summer months Wayne Crumpler was drag racing on Highway 117. He pulled over to get back into his lane, lost control of his car, ran off the road and hit a tree so hard it popped the top out. He died instantly.

It has been over 50 years since I first entered the halls of Charles B. Aycock. Until I started writing my story and seeing it on paper, I didn't realize just how broken and fractured I was. I was all crumbled up inside. I had no self-esteem. I put on a good front, and even talked about my experiences at Charles B. Aycock with my sisters from time to time, but the pain was still there. In the Bible, Scripture says you must forgive those who have done you wrong before you can begin to heal.

Did you know that in the Bible the word *Forgive* is written 38 times?

And in the New Testament the word *Forgiveness* is written 146 times?

Here are four Scriptures I have for you:

MARK 11:25-26

25 And when ye stand praying, forgive, if ye have ought against any; that your Father also which is in heaven may forgive you your trespasses.

26 But if ye do not forgive, neither will your Father which is in heaven forgive your trespasses.

EPHESIANS 5:31-32

31 Let all bitterness, and wrath, and anger, and clamour, and evil speaking, be put away from you, with all malice:

32 And be ye kind one to another, tenderhearted, forgiving one another, even as God for Christ's sake hath forgiven you.

I want to take this opportunity to thank The Executive Team and Norwayne Alumni for giving me a chance to share my story with you. May God continue Blessing you for the wonderful works you're doing.

Trusting GOD, Even Unto Death

Revelation 1:18 (KJV) states. "I am He that liveth, and was dead; and behold, I am alive for evermore, Amen; and have the keys of hell and death." It is because of Christ's tomb experience and coming forth a conqueror, victorious and with the promise of eternal life for each of us that I can trust GOD, even unto death.

The human mind cannot fully comprehend life and death, yet for both, the Word of God gives adequate promises and understanding. The Bible is our roadmap to living an abundant life on this earth and preparation for the life to come. There are scriptures to give us solace and comfort as we are faced with all forms of death, albeit sudden death, death because of wars, long termed illnesses, and the myriad of other causes of death. That said, in my opinion, I know that there is no way to explain or fully understand life, let alone death, which will always be a mystery.

With the emergence of COVID-19 in late 2019 and the shutdown of the entire world during March 2020, the preceding months continue to be rough as the virus and variants spreads rampant and the death toll to date in the United States alone reaches over 800,000. The world's population was forced to rethink every aspect of life - interaction with each other, isolation from family and friends, church worship; work environment, shopping, school/college attendance; travel – no aspect of daily life has been left untouched.

Death invaded my life at an early age with the demise of infant brothers. Being young, death did not register and was not something that was freely discussed in the home. At age 13, I experienced a deep loss when my maternal grandmother died after a short illness. During that time, families had viewings in their home and people came to pay their respect. This was my first recollection of hearing sayings like, "She/He is in a better place now;" "She/He is no longer in pain;"

"She/He is now in heaven;" or "She/He is looking down or smiling down on us."

Satan being the deceiver that he is, has since the beginning of time filled the human mind with deception and falsehood about God, life, and death.

As the days turned into months and the months into years, I have experienced other deaths. Death of classmates, best friends, aunts, uncles, grandparents, cousins, neighbors, church members, co-workers, sister, brother and father in-law, and parents, etc. that have impacted my life. Each death has left a profound void that only God's infinite grace and mercy have sustained my sanity and well-being.

It is through understanding Biblical truths about life and death that I have been able to find a sense of peace with loss of loved ones and others during my lifetime. It is those Biblical truths that have answered plaguing questions about what happens when we die, the state of the dead, the resurrection of Christ and His soon return.

As I write this, I understand that even now, I have eternal life (I John 5:11 and John 3:16 (KJV). When we believe, we have life; because God gives it to us, but that eternal life is kept in heaven and that life is in God's Son. So, when Jesus returns that "eternal life" becomes my possession as well as the possession of all believers. Colossians 3:3 (KJV) tells us that when we die our life is hid with Christ in God. According to Colossians 3:4 (KJV), our real life is in Christ and when he appears, then I/you too will appear with Him and share His glory. Immortality will be to those who have died in Christ and those who are still alive and believe in Christ at Jesus' second coming (1 Corinthians 15:51-54 and John 6:55 KJV). Until that great waking up day, all who have died wait in the grave. At the last trumpet sound, we will possess immortality (I Thessalonians 4:13 15-17 KJV).

Over and over the scriptures describe death as sleep. "For the Lord himself will descend from heaven with a cry of command, with the archangel's call, and with the sound of the trumpet of God. And the dead in Christ will rise first; then we who are alive, who are left shall be caught up together with them in the clouds to meet the Lord in the air; and so, we shall always be with the Lord."

It is good news to know that the dead in Christ have not preceded us to heaven, nor will individuals alive in Christ at His second coming precede the dead to heaven. All individuals who are righteous at Christ's second coming, both dead and alive, will go to heaven together.

The Bible is clear that in death we do not know anything. According to Psalms 146:6 (KJV), "when a man dies his breath goeth forth, he returneth to the earth; in that very day his thoughts perish;" and Ecclesiastes 9:5 indicates, "the living know that they shall die; but the dead know not anything." "Their love, their hatred is perished, and they don't know anything that goes on under the sun." Other text that substantiates this belief includes Job 14:21, Psalm 6:5, KJV).

Genesis 2:2 (KJV) states that God formed man from the dust of the ground, breathed into his nostrils the breath of life, and man became a living soul. It is at death, that unconscious sleep, when the breath of life goes back to God (Ecclesiastes 12:7 (KNV).

For all God's blessings and the goodness bestowed upon my life, I am eternally grateful. It has been through cultivating an intimate relationship with Jesus and faith in God's word that I have been able to endure the pain, loneliness, rejection, separation, betrayal, heartache, racism, sickness, death etc., that have invaded my life. For me, everything on this earth is worth NOTHING compared to the awaiting glory prepared in heaven by my SAVIOUR (John 14:1-4).

Oh, how I look forward to the day when Christ is seen by every eye breaking through the clouds in all His glory to redeem His people (Revelation 1:7). I await Revelation 21:1-4, a new heaven, and a new earth, where there will be no more crying, nor pain, for the former things will be passed away (Revelation 21:1-4). No more earthquakes, floods, famine, tornadoes, hurricanes, and especially funerals.

It gives my heart hope and peace, because as Jesus said, "Lazarus, come forth, (John 11:38-44), one day if I am asleep in Christ's righteousness, I too can hear those words, "Linda, come forth." So, "Come, Lord Jesus." (Revelation 22:12-21 KJV).

Van Jewell Sampson Marshall   *Norwayne Class of 1969*

JAMES and BET

Building Character and Unleashing Potential

In three days, two weather fronts moved through. The first one swept in and brought with it a fierce southeastern storm. Not the steamy, thunder crashing, and lightning striking storms that we had grown accustomed to in the deep south, but an eerie, cold, and at the onset, a loud and still winter storm. The wind howled around the corners of the house making sounds like the cries of a wounded animal. Windows rattled in their panes and brisk air seeped through cracks around the sills that made their plastic coverings look like they were breathing.

The freezing rain began before sunrise and in the light of the day seemed to colorlessly cascade from an empty sky. The rain formed into ice, coating everything it touched as quickly as it landed. The layers of ice rapidly and thickly covered the tops of the barn and the outhouse, the needles of the silenced pines, the leafless trees, the berried holly bushes, and the grass that had long ago turned brown. It coated the walkways and the red flagged mailbox at the side of the impassable road in sparkling icy splendor. I recall being frequently drawn to the window by the awesomeness of the ice coated world. It started to warm up later that day; the sun came out and the ice began to melt. The next morning's sun and above freezing temperature returned the earth to normal as abruptly as it had changed.

I am going to digress here to acquaint you with the people, places and things in this story. Hopefully you will see the building of character and the unleashing of potential. And also, how tumultuous storms or upsets can serve to complete moments in the joys of life's fullness.

At that time, my parents only had eight children. Our baby sister, the ninth child, my mother's change of life miracle, came six years later, slightly over a year after the birth of my son, Rahji, their first grandchild. My youngest brother had been born that fall and my oldest brother was a high school junior. Between them, five girls and another son, the seventh child, were born.

We came like steps on a ladder, my mother often said. We all had been born about two years apart except for the fifth child which gave her a four-year birthing break and the seventh which granted three. Birth control was either unconsidered or thought to be ungodly and the rhythm method had seemingly worked mostly as a pulsating cadence to baby generating sex. She told us that she would conceal her pregnancies as long as she could because as soon as the fruit of their intimacy began to show, she had to brace herself to hear over and over, *"Lord, Sis Bet!!! You pregnant again!!!???"* She'd inescapably reply, *"Yes, I'm pregnant again!"* Sometimes, depending on who it was and the degree of maliciousness she perceived, she would even add, *"And, I enjoyed every moment of it!"*

As she strutted away, she'd turn to look back and catch the busybody women's mouths dropped open in disbelief and surprise. She was not a cussing woman but sometimes a few other choice words for that failing rhythm method, and the people, crossed her mind though. Then, she would curb those hateful thoughts and lovingly caress her swollen belly and smile both in remembrance of what was and anticipation of her soon to come bundle of joy.

As many babies as our parents had, amazingly, they managed to shield us from the sight and sounds of their passion. We were really very sheltered and underexposed. Yet, we were so protected from much of the world's chaos.

I started school the 1957 – 1958 year at *Pikeville Training School*. I was familiar with the school house building because it was across the road and down the railroad tracks from *Elm Grove Church,* the

93

Pikeville *Colored* community church that my family attended. I can't remember whether or not I was eager to go to school. I do remember feeling excitement as I walked up the steps of the school house and how the classroom, though filled with children and books and desks, seemed so empty when I entered.

During my school years, I had some really great teachers that had mastered the art of teaching and that seemed to love educating that I really liked and tried to model myself after. I had some awful teachers, too, that functioned as if they hated what they did and that probably would not even have been considered jacks of the trade that I wished I could have wished away. Some teachers even had an insensitive stabbing and prying way of asking questions or generating conversations that would publicly disclose the students' home way of life.

Example. In health class, teachers taught us proper nutrition and healthy eating habits from the *7 Basic Food Group Chart*, the precursor to the ninety's *Food Pyramid* and President Barack Obama Administration's *MyPlate.* The chart stated that to protect yourself from illnesses you should eat something from each group daily. Teachers would unmindfully follow the handed-down, not-written-for low-income American Blacks health book teaching prompts, and give the low-income American Black students class assignments like *Write Down What You Had for Dinner Last Night!*

Mother cooked hearty meals and made biscuits for Daddy *every* day, but very, very seldom would our meals (even on Sundays when we usually had fried chicken with seasonal fruit and vegetables and cakes or pies in abundance) satisfy more than five of the food groups. Often, dried black-eyed peas or pinto beans *was* the meat group, since fat back and streak of lean chunks didn't count as a healthy meat choice. Fortunately, since we didn't have a television and I read anything readable I could get my hands on, I was able to produce a meal on paper that not only "packed a punch", as promoted in the text books, but that also generated an excellent grade.

I *must* add that during hunting season, Daddy, who was an expert shooter, regularly came home with the pockets of his hunting jacket filled to overflow with buck shot laden rabbits, squirrels and birds. I didn't include those in my assignment because, be that meat as it may, game meat had not yet come to be called a *delicacy*. And, no such bloody and unclean things were displayed in the textbooks.

Even though our home cooked meals weren't extravagant, we were never hungry. The whole family ate supper together every evening. Daddy would give thanks and say blessings and grace. Each week Mother made all of us memorize a verse of scripture and recite it daily after grace in a round table fashion. Only the preschoolers could quote short verses like *"Jesus wept," "Rejoice evermore,"* or *"Pray without ceasing"* which she taught them to help develop their speech and language skills.

And, as if teachers were trying to find out which homes had a television, or so I perceived in my dread, they would assign the class to watch the evening news and write about one of the day's current events. Blessed with a vivid imagination, I would carefully listen to the news on our radio and make up and write my own visual effects. *Or,* teachers would assign us to clip a newspaper article and expound on it. Our home was void of newspapers too. Surely, teachers had not always lived in a home where their families subscribed to newspapers and magazines, I mused. Were they not once, somewhere down their line, without running water toilets and toilet tissue but fated to use the pages of an old *Sears and Roebuck* mail order catalog stashed in the outhouse corner, its black and white pages softened by prolonged rubbing, to wipe their backsides in the outhouse? *chuckle, chuckle*

And though not having a television was our mother's way of shielding us from derogatory worldly influences, she also valued and continuously sought ways to expand our breadth of knowledge. She denied our whines for a television with, "Read a book." That, however, caused us to excel in class and to be considered and remembered as exceptionally sharp, smart and bright.

Lastly, after summer break, the inevitable and inevitably unwanted essay theme was always *What You Did or Where You Went During Summer Vacation.* Ironically, I got a thrill out of telling the White people, whom we worked *for* and *with*, putting in *their* tobacco during the summer about the delightful day of fun our church had congregating at the Umstead State Park in Raleigh when they shared tales about their weekend family drive to the Smoky Mountains. That delight somehow drastically dwindled when asked by one of my teachers to read my usually well-written assignment aloud in class following peers whose essays about their summer ventures provoked *ooohs* and *aaahs* because they had traveled so much farther and done so much more.

Actually, we looked forward to and saved our spending money from putting in tobacco for our summer trip where we could congregate and feel on top of the world. Where one could eat as many grilled hot dogs and hamburgers and chips and drink as much soda pop and Julip as their stomachs could hold. Where children seemed to play without getting tired. Where young lovers sneaked off to steal kisses; and cigarette smokers, if they could find some chewing gum, to take two or three quick puffs. Where the wearied lines in the faces of the older folks gave way to lines of laughter. Where there was joy in the air, and everything felt all right and people felt empowered and worry free. *At least for a day.*

Before enrolling in school, the church was just about our only social outlet. We went to Sunday School *every* Sunday. Mother would starch and iron our handmade clothes, which were so well tailored that today they would be labeled custom made, on Saturday evening. She'd plait our hair, readying our braids that she had trained to be long and thick, for Sunday's colorful ribbons. Daddy would cut and edge the boys' hair; crease press their pants and polish all of our shoes or add a special shine to the girls' using one of Mother's hot breakfast biscuits if we wore patent leather. If a sole came loose, he'd heat and spread a glue concoction to reattach it, and place it under the weight of a leg of mother's Singer pedal sewing machine to bond.

Often, after ripping about and running around playing with friends at school or church, by the time you walked that quarter of a mile from home and back on that dirt road, that glue gave way, and that old shoe sole would be flop, flop, flopping again. The evening would find that same shoe stuck with a fresh glob of smelly glue and back under the machine leg. Frequently that sole's new beginning came to the same bad end the next day.

Our parents trained us to live by the Golden Rule: *Do unto others only what you would have them do unto you.* As funny as it is to see somebody's step slip or a falling body frantically flailing through the air, we weren't allowed to laugh when somebody stumbled and fell. "You should always show concern that your brother or your sister hasn't been injured," chastised our mother, "And instead of laughing, you should have asked did you hurt yourself?" We got in trouble many a times for snickering out that question, while barely able to hold our laughter. I later read that neurology suggests that when we see someone's feet literally coming from under them, with their hands waving and arms flying, mirror neurons in our brains make us feel as if we are the ones precariously tumbling and that subconscious mental picture provokes us to react with laughter. *hehehehe*

We also never went to bed without saying to our parents and everybody near them, *"Good night. I hope you have a good night's rest."* And they, as well as everybody that heard you would reply, *"Thanks. I hope you the same."*

Though we were poor and didn't have much in the material sense, our parents' approach to life, with all of its cares and complications, was amazingly simple because they recognized and relied on God in their own, individual ways. They seemed to have a way of making life shine brightly so that our poverty was never grinding.

Adolescence and peer comparison, however, marched in and feelings of shame not only began to foster a loathing of my parents' strict ways and teachings but also caused me to forget the astronomical struggles they braved and the extreme sacrifices they had made to keep us together as a family unit. Perhaps it was the anxiety of puberty that magnified the disappointment of *not having things*, like a car or television or an inside toilet and having to wear the same pair of dime store loafers from the first day of school until we were able to get a new pair of Hush Puppies for Christmas, *and things*. Or maybe it was because I was getting older and could sense emotions that I was in the past unable to detect. Or possibly the ever-growing and constantly changing needs and demands of the older four of us were beginning to transfer negative energies. Perchance, time was merely taking its toll.

Nonetheless, the stress and frustration that accompanies lack were starting to cause wordless tension in our home. I could detect the dissatisfaction in Mother's voice, as she was busy sewing or cooking or something and she'd remind Daddy, "James we *really* need such and such" or "We are out of this or that; we've been out of it for a good while now." And the annoyance in his reply, "Bet, I'm doing the best I can. You can't get blood out of a turnip!" or "You can't fit Goldsboro inside of Pikeville!" He'd then pick up his guitar and go out on the porch and begin to sing, rather than his usual gospel quartet tunes, songs like *If It Ain't One Thing I Declare It's Another.*

I hope that this digression of acquaintance was like breaking bread with old friends and recollecting. Let us now get back to the wintry storms and the end of this tale...

By the year of the storms, we no longer walked to school. My family had moved from the house on the dusty road which was called *The Alley* until it was later paved and named *Booker Street*. We lived in a big unpainted house on a hill way out in the country with a giant oak tree by the water pump in our front yard. All of Pikeville's Black youth were then being bused to *Norwayne School*, which had recently been built for people labeled *Colored,* in neighboring Fremont.

We always had a garden but our garden space was now the size of a little field. We had a big chest freezer, so Mother was able to freeze enough fresh vegetables to last through the winter. We even had a chicken coop and Daddy went to the hatchery and purchased over a hundred biddies, or so it seemed. We soon were gathering eggs and dressing fryers for meals. We had hogs then too. Daddy and my brother had built a pen off from the house near the woods. When the wind blew from that direction though, sometimes we still smelled its stench.

The second front raced up from the south and sent temperatures plunging to below freezing. Daddy and my brother had gone to the pigsty when the freezing rain started to make sure the enclosure was steady and the bedding was clean and dry because a sow had recently farrowed a large litter. When they returned, they brought in extra wood and coal out of the ice for the potbellied and kitchen stoves. The fires were burning at full blast. The house was nice and toasty.

We had just finished supper. Daddy might have been strumming his guitar or nodding, and Mother was more than likely reading her Bible or sewing. I don't remember what we were doing. We might have been eating peanuts since Mother or Daddy would often roast a pan in the evening while the oven was still hot. There were so many of us that there was always plenty of activity going on in our house. That could have factored into why us older girls read so much; we were seeking solitude.

A startling scream suddenly shattered the air followed by grunts, squeals, and more screams.

"I hope ain't no devilish animal done got to them hogs," Daddy said. "Something's got 'em scared."

They never cussed in front of us and didn't allow us to use curse words. "Devilish" pronounced *devlish* and "shit" pronounced *sheeit* were Daddy's favorite expletives, while "*Well, Praise the Lord*" and "*God loves you*" were Mother's words of choice.

Daddy was a man of truth and no nonsense who had a low tolerance for the pretense and putting-on of others and would say "shit on it" in a minute, in dismissal of foolishness, while Mother's sense of integrity and desire to portray that one person is as good as the next caused castaways, like our loving alcoholic cousin couple or people that struggled with their identity or anything else, to feel worthwhile. People were always giving her things, and she would always show appreciation for the thought and receive their gifts with gracious kindness. Often, they were treasures, yet sometimes they were only fit to be used as quilting scraps or discarded. It did not matter; if *anybody* gave her *anything*, they left her feeling *righteous* about their good deed.

Daddy and my brother quickly put on their coats and hats and grabbed both the shotgun and the rifle and headed towards the woods. Mother hastened us out of the windows' view and away from the disturbing sounds. She calmed our fears and apprehension by explaining how animals were vulnerable like us, and how they, also like us, cry when they are hurting.

Fortunately, we heard no gunshots, but the hogs seemed to have gone wild. *Endlessly.*

Soon, after what seemed like forever, the back door opened, and Daddy shouted for Mother to keep the children back but to come to the kitchen because he needed her help. She instructed my oldest sister to read a story to the others and called me alongside to assist them.

Daddy and my brother both had strained looks on their faces. My brother was carrying a batch of fresh straw and Daddy was holding one of the suckling pigs, whose continuous squeal was so weak that you could barely hear it, in blood-soaked straw in his arms. He laid the piglet on a baby blanket that my mother had placed on a side table. Its stomach was split open, and its intestines were sticking out.

Daddy said, "That sow accidentally stepped on her pig and her hoof tore him up. We've got to clean him, get his guts back in and sew him up or he's going to die."

Orders and instructions started to fly. Hot water from the kitchen stove reservoir, rags cut from an old white cotton sheet, scissors, a large needle, alcohol for sterilization, twine, a spool of black thread, a baby bottle with a special formula and an old nipple emerged. Under a lamp with the shade removed so it could give extra light, on a side table in the kitchen, Daddy and Mother performed surgery, fed, and saved the life of a little pig.

There are hidden jewels in doing good and also in seeing and recognizing the good in others. "I just about had to kill that old sow to get to that pig," Daddy chuckled as they finished cleaning up from the emergency surgery. "She was dangerous. *Fierce.* She was determined that nothing was going to get to her little squealing pigs. She reminded me of you Bet."

Mother nodded her head and smiled a great big smile. "That was an extraordinary and real good thing that you just did James," she complimented.

I saw the spark that connected them fizzing. I was reminded then, and at times like that, that it is not about cars or televisions or running water or flopping shoes or any tangible thing. It became clear to me that God places within us a bit of Himself in ways that surpasses all understanding. Life, and that more abundantly. *Then I wondered if there would be another step added to intimacy's ladder that night.*

Unfortunately for the pig and good for us, the next year at hog killing time, that *saved* pig became one of the *slaughtered.* Each winter, the neighbors gathered at each other's homes for butchering in rotation. The men slew and bled the hogs, singed and scraped their hair, gutted and cut the hogs into parts, and began the saltpeter curing rub. The women chopped, ground, and seasoned the meat for sausage, washed and stuffed the intestines used for casing, cooked the skins and fat that the men had thrown into the iron kettles down to lard and cracklings, and prepared a feast to reward everybody at finishing time. *Ironically*, that little pig lived and was fattened up to meet the meat requirement of the *7 Basic Food Group Chart* in many and numerous forms.

Just before dusk, it started to snow. We didn't get to see snow much, so we stood at the windows and watched the falling flakes as long as we could make them out. North Carolina had not yet adopted *Daylight Savings Time*, so it didn't get dark as early during the winter months. The youngsters had never even seen accumulating snow, only flurries. This was the first snow of the season, so our hopes were that it would be deep enough for Daddy to find enough clean snow in the middle for Mother to make us some snow cream. They said that the snow closest to the ground was unusable because it was dirty from the earth and cleaning the atmosphere and that the top layer had to be put aside because of potential droppings from the element and animals.

All of our hopes came to be!

The next morning, we woke up to a world with more snow than we had ever seen in our lives. Daddy, who always was up before the roosters crowed, had gone out to check the animals. We watched him trudging through the snow, being careful to step around the edges of the field, so as not to disturb the area that would soon become our playground. Mother was cooking breakfast and promised that we could go out to play in the snow as soon as everybody ate and we cleaned up the kitchen.

Girls didn't wear pants back then, so Mother had us to put on two or three pairs of skin tights to help protect our legs from the wet cold. Only our oldest brother had need for boots because of hunting and fishing, so Daddy helped us wrap our feet, ankles and legs with leftover plastic he'd used on the windows to shut out the winter's draft to help ward off the wet snow. He then swaddled my younger brother, who was a toddler that was certain to do a lot of falling in that deep snow, up like a little plastic mummy.

We didn't have a regular need for gloves nor scarves either, since it seldom snowed and was usually not very cold, so Mother had us to don our hats, put socks on our hands, wrap an extra piece of clothing around our necks like a scarf and tuck it inside our not-made-for-cold-snowy-weather winter coats and we headed outside with Daddy to play in the snow. We laughed! And fell! And rolled in the snow! And threw handfuls up in the air! We tasted the snow and made snowballs and snow angels! We built a *gigantic* snowman! That frosty snowman with his holly berried hat lingered in an ever melting and disfiguring state for a long, long time after the earth warmed and the snow on the ground disappeared.

Daddy had built up the fires in the wood stove and both heaters so the whole house would be toasty warm for us to change clothes when we came in. Mother had laid out clothes for the younger four. She collected our wet clothing and Daddy placed our soggy shoes near the base of the heaters to dry out. After we thawed our hands in a pail of warm water, we all sat around the heaters and held our then throbbing fingers and shivery toes as close to the fire as we could stand to bring them back to life.

Once everybody was dry, warm, and cozy, the snow cream talk began. *"Can we have some snow cream now?"* was becoming an incessant chant. *"Daddy... Mother... Daddy ... Mother ..."*

So, Daddy went outside to gather up snow and Mother began making the sugar, vanilla flavoring, milk and cream filling to mix with it.

My sisters and I set out bowls and spoons at everybody's seat at the table in great anticipation. Of course, Mother let us taste the mixture like she always did with her batter when she made cakes. The sweet concoction was so delicious even without the snow; *we could only imagine*. And, yes, we finally went to *snow cream heaven*!

The snow was still there the next day, still marvelously white and fluffy looking, but for me the novelty of newness and excitement of touch had worn off, and I was satisfied to indirectly enjoy its magnificence from the warmth of the house. The little ones, however, were anxious to go outside again, never minding getting all wet and cold. So, of course, we older ones had to go outside with the younger ones to watch over and play with them. And as it often happens when you put your reserves aside and do something that you are unwilling to do, we found just as much pleasure in doing it as they did.

Daddy went inside with the baby this time so Mother came out to join us. She had crumbled up leftover biscuits to feed the birds. "They are bound to be hungry since the snow has covered up what they usually find to eat," she told us. "Let's put the crumbs down in the shape of a great big heart," she said. Afterwards she added, "The snowbirds won't come for the food we put down while we are out here, but when we leave and go inside, they'll come. Let's go in the house and watch. When they all pitch down to eat, it's going to look like an artist drew a magnificent heart in the snow." How easily she redirected the youngsters' thought process and persuaded them to come in out of the cold. It was good that she relieved us of that task.

That night we all had a good night's rest indeed. That's the way we lived. That's the way we loved. That's the way we learned.

James and Bet were two strong and remarkable beings.

My brothers often recount tales Daddy told them while he was teaching them to hunt and fish. He didn't work as a brick layer because the last requirement of the training program required men to work and live away from home and family was too important for that.

Daddy loved baseball. One of his league pitchers said that Daddy was the best catcher a pitcher could ask for. He had to leave the team because the team usually played double headers on Sundays and Daddy couldn't make it to the first game on time. Like a lot of players, his parents insisted that he go to church before playing ball on the *Lord's Day*. And his daddy was a church deacon, *too*. He had stopped school after the sixth grade to help with farm work, yet he understood how the universe behaved and the properties of metals and could understand those sections in my older sister's college chemistry and physics books. Neither did we find out as young adults, like some cousins on *both* sides of our family, that some of the very girls we had grown up with and played with as friends *were our very own siblings*! He fathered no children outside of the marriage.

Mother was just about as smart as they come, too. The girls can relate tales she shared as she deepened our knowledge and shaped our understanding of the world by transferring her love of nature and reading to us. She skipped a grade in school and although her classmates presumed she was the student who would receive the one annual scholarship that was offered for teacher's college, she was quite dark-skinned, so the coveted scholarship was granted to a presumed better suited light-skinned girl instead. She had a special gift for mothering too; she taught us our colors, shapes, numbers, alphabets, and lettering long before we started school. She taught us how to read, cook, sew and how to tend the yard and garden. We watched and helped her can fruits and vegetables and make pickles. She helped us with our homework and had us memorize poetry for school and church recitals and taught us all the books of the Bible.

Both of them must have often been anguished by thoughts of their many missed opportunities, but they were determined to do the right thing and kept on sacrificing for us and each other. Beyond providing food, shelter, and comfort, they demonstrated kindness, supplied guidance, patterned principles, taught us wisdom and braved reproaches for us. They freely gave unto us the *Gift of Love,* the greatest gift a human being can receive.

Like the winter storms, *James, Jr. and Geneva "Bet" Coley Sampson* are long gone. The first of their nine children are now *the old folks* and the younger ones are rapidly approaching that milestone. Hopefully, the world *has* and *will* continue to experience *James and Bet* through the best of us, their offspring. And ours. And theirs…

The Nine of Us

Jimmy Ray
Myra Juanita
Van Jewel
Rosilyn Elnora
Teresa Ann
Jan Symanthia
Danny Stewart
Randy James
Davonka Yvette

Erma Jean Smith-King, PhD, MBA, MPH, RN, CNE,
ACUE   Charles B. Aycock   Class of 1970

My Story

Growing up in a low wealth tenant farming family in Northern Wayne County did not dampen my dreams or aspirations. As I reflect on my early childhood in Pikeville without the amenities of indoor plumbing, electrical heat, and such, my grandparents, Arthur and Rena Smith, reared me safely and provided caring and love to surmount the obstacles and challenges that are part of life.

In addition to the unconditional love and support of my grandparents and other family members and neighbors, the influence of Pikeville Training School and Norwayne School grounded my pursuit for lifelong learning in my early development. Even though segregation was the law of the land, the old adage, "don't let your circumstances define you," permeated the culture of the schools and kept my eye on the prize. I was poor but I was not downtrodden. I was poor and no one minimized my dreams. In fact, the realization of the serious nature of my poorness occurred in a sociology class at NC A&T in 1971 while discussing the federal poverty guidelines. When I saw the income level for a family of four in poverty, I gasped in disbelief, and said, "Wow, I lived in abject poverty!" The yearly income for a family of four in 1971 was a whopping $4,137! My grandparents probably made less than that as tenant farmers BUT the caring and love they showered on me replaced the absence of greenbacks. I believe that success is possible in a supportive and loving environment. Jean Watson, a notable nursing theorist, says that "caring regenerates life energies and potentiates our capabilities."

Pikeville Training School – 1st to 3rd Grade

Norwayne School – 4th to 9th Grade

Charles B. Aycock High School – 10th to 12th grade

NC A&T State University – 1974, BSN

University of North Carolina at Chapel Hill – 1977, MPH

Meredith College – 1990, MBA

NC A&T State University – 2012 – PhD

Tar in My Soul

I am Sherree Denise Sutton, born at Wayne Memorial Hospital, Goldsboro and grew up in Faro and Eureka, North Carolina. My brother, Frankie and I were raised by my maternal grandmother and grandfather. I attended Norwayne School for the first nine years of my primary education. For those that do not know, North Carolina is known as the Tar Heel State; due to the high production of tar, pitch, and turpentine. This story is a look inside family life in the rural south. God's mercy, grace, and favor, family, work, church, community, and my determination to place no limits on myself, made me who I am.

Another 4:30 a.m. start to the day! The tobacco is cured, and the barn needs to be cleared for the next round—so up and at 'em.

It is still dark but duty calls. My duty is to pass the sticks of bundled, cured tobacco down to my brother, Frankie, standing on the dirt floor of the barn. He will stack them on a trailer for transport to the pack house. Climbing the tier poles in the barn has become part of my seasonal routine when "putting in tobacco" as we called it. My tree-climbing skills prepared me for this role. Trees were my refuge when I needed to hide from my grandmother and her endless list of chores. I always loved to read, so I would take a book, climb the large oak in the front yard and read for hours. Until my legs were long enough to allow me to straddle the tier poles, my brother would pass me a wood plank to stand on. My grandfather had measured the plank to ensure it would be long enough to cover the length between the tiers to serve as my platform so that I would not fall.

As a farmer's granddaughter, there is no time for girly stuff—from March until September, these six months are set aside for planting and harvesting the crops. We grew corn, cotton, and tobacco. I must admit, I was one happy child when my grandfather decided to stop growing cotton. There was absolutely no love lost by me. I was so tired of dragging a burlap sack down cotton rows in 90+ degree weather—not to mention the burs tearing up my fingers. By the time my brother and I were ten and twelve years old, cotton was no longer on our crop list.

We participated in every step of the process of growing tobacco--a very labor-intensive process. I remember it like it was yesterday. The process of growing and harvesting tobacco spans six months of the year. The first step is bedding the seeds—sowing seeds in a constructed seed bed. Two months later, the plants have grown and are strong enough to continue growing in a field. A field can range in size from one acre to numerous acres.

We were responsible for transplanting each plant by hand, using what is called a peg. A peg is a wood object usually one to two inches thick, with a curve at the top and a pointed tip. The pointed tip is thrust into the soil to create an opening to place the plant. This step in the process is known as setting out tobacco. Once the planting was complete, the rows of plants were tended, which included fertilizing, applying pesticides—when necessary, and watering. These steps of the process were intended to maximize the quality and yield of the crop.

Our family of five—grandfather, grandmother, uncle, my brother, and me—were the primary workforce responsible for completing the first stages of bringing a crop to harvest. Grandma did not always participate in all the steps because most of her time was spent cooking for the family and taking care of all the other household tasks.

Like cotton, working with tobacco left its mark too. My brother and I had deep tans at the end of summer that the average Caucasian would be envious of. We also started the school year with yellow stains on the palms of our hands, along with callouses; and oftentimes blisters on the sides of our hands.

Competitiveness was ingrained in both my brother and I from an early age. We were always expected to "outdo" one another in the tasks we were responsible for. I now realize that was the adults' way of increasing our productivity. The use of competition was not only used to result in the highest level of productivity from us, but from everyone working during harvest time.

When cotton was still on the crop list, we were challenged to pick the highest number of pounds for the day. Each burlap sack we filled, granddad weighed it and at the end of the day, he would tell us the total pounds picked for the day. I was usually at the lower end of the production list. I simply hated the task and the faster I tried to pick, the greater the damage to my hands.

I redeemed myself by stepping up my game working in tobacco. Once the plants had grown to a respectable height and begun to flower, it was time for the step in the process called "topping" or what some referred to as "suckering" tobacco. Simply put, we had to break off the tops of the tobacco stalk where the flowers were located. This step allowed the plant to continue to grow and fully mature, yielding taller plants with larger leaves.

Frankie and I often turned the task into a game and always a competition. We would start at the end of our row at the same time and whomever finished first, granddad declared the winner. Of course, our grandfather inspected our work to determine if it had been done properly. Both of us were guilty of damaging a few stalks because we could not reach the tops of stalks while attempting to speed, resulting in breaking leaves or breaking entire stalks.

During our childhood, in the decades of the sixties and early seventies, tobacco was like gold to farmers—so damaging stalks was not a wise thing to do. I also learned to loop bundles of tobacco at a respectable speed.

While we were always at work during daylight hours, we managed to turn our tasks into our version of fun. We were children. There were many days when both of us missed school. We had to stay home to

111

work on the farm; and silly us, we thought we could hide from our neighbors that rode the same bus with us. When we would see the bus round the curve near our house, we would lie face down in the rows. I know, silly, but it was representative of our childhood simplicity and innocence.

We would oftentimes leave the house at dawn and after completing the task of clearing the barn, return to a hot, home-cooked meal. Grandma was up before everyone else and had a full breakfast waiting when we got back—usually in the 6 a.m.- 6:30 a.m. timeframe. We had to return to work after breakfast for the start of the actual workday. I remember those meals fondly. She would make buttermilk biscuits, from scratch, along with bacon or sausage, eggs, and grits. I was not a fan of grits but there was always molasses. My grandfather raised pigs, so the bacon and sausage came from our smokehouse.

A smokehouse is a small building, usually built out of wood, where the pork is cured. The pork—hams, shoulders, sausage, etc. is hung from the ceiling; after being rubbed in salt, pepper, and other spices to preserve it. My grandmother was known for her sausage-making skills in our community, as well as her overall cooking and baking skills.

Mid-day, we would take a break for dinner (now known as lunch) and that meal would consist of items like corn bread or biscuits, fried chicken, stewed beef, rice and gravy or mashed potatoes, collard greens, string beans, okra, or cabbage. All the food was produced on the farm, except the ingredients for the biscuits and cornbread and the rice. The last meal of the day, supper (now known as dinner) was also a full meal, consisting of items like pork chops, liver, barbecue chicken or pork, sweet potatoes, etc. I absolutely refused to eat liver and unlike a child of today, there was no alternative prepared for me. My grandmother's rule was we ate what she cooked or went without. Supper on Friday always included some type of fish, usually fried.

112

The memory of third Sunday church services, also known as Quarterly Meeting, always brings a smile to my face. We were Baptist and the third Sunday service was an all-day service and referred to as Quarterly Meeting. My grandmother would start cooking on Friday afternoon to prepare the food she would take to church on those Sundays. Her cakes and pies were always made from scratch. She would fill the trunk of our car with boxes of food—baked or fried chicken, barbeque or a baked ham, collard greens, her world-class potato salad, coleslaw, hushpuppies, and a minimum of two cakes or other desserts. Church members would always come to the car before we could unload the food for her—asking what she had cooked. It was like one big family reunion or picnic. All the church mothers and sisters would bring food and place it on a long picnic-type table to be shared with everyone. During the fall and winter, everyone moved inside to the church dining hall. My grandmother's food would disappear as soon as it was placed on the table. Most people would bring one or two dishes or desserts, but my grandmother always took the full Sunday dinner.

During those times, children were to be seen and not heard. Some also believed adults were to be served first and children should wait. My brother and I were not fans of this practice. We would pout throughout the afternoon service because there was something that we did not get to eat from our grandmother's contributions—usually dessert or one of our favorite dishes. We were not allowed, nor did we want to eat the food contributed by other ladies unless they were someone my grandmother knew well.

I loved to get dressed up in what was known as church clothes, but only on Sunday. Grandma usually starched my dresses to perfection and there was always a crinoline slip underneath. Grandma was a girly-girl so there was a ribbon on every plat of my hair, lace trim on my socks and rows of lace on my underwear. While I loved the pretty dresses, I absolutely hated all the frills. I was a card-carrying tomboy and Sunday was the only day you would see me in a dress, except during the school year. In the winter months I got to wear pants to school but under my dresses and would have to take them off when I got to school. Girls could not wear pants in school in those days. Climbing trees, riding my bicycle or a good foot race were not activities that could be done comfortably while wearing a dress, but they were my favorite activities.

By the end of the day, or before the end of morning service, my brother's tie would be in his pocket, his shirt hanging out and shoes scuffed or full of sand. He would manage to feign having to go to the bathroom and wind up outside with the other boys. My grandfather, Frank, was a deacon, but he seemed to have outside duty often and would see my brother sneaking outside. Sometimes he allowed him to stay outside. It was one of the benefits of being male in those days.

My grandfather believed in teaching both of us how to do things at an early age. For example, he gave me driving lessons before I could reach the brake and gas pedals—that explains my life-long love affair with cars. In our community and beyond, he was known for his love of cars and driving fast. Age never hindered him from accepting a challenge from one of the young boys in the area. Little did they know, he would not back down from a race he knew he was going to win. His cars were his prize possessions, and he made a habit of trading up every couple of years. He was a Ford man. I thought for sure he was going to do damage to my uncle when he wrecked one of his new cars. It was a sky-blue Ford. He had just bought it, when he let my uncle, and one of his friends use it one night to go to a basketball game. My uncle flipped the car over a brick-wall, and it landed in the schoolyard in Eureka. They both walked away without injury. Granddad replaced the car with another one, identical to the first one. He had the reputation of being as tough as nails and we were all shocked when my uncle did not incur granddad's wrath. His main concern was that he and Johnny (my uncle's friend) walked away unscathed. I think seeing the condition of the car scared him so much, he had no time for anger.

My driving skills were honed on a tractor—one of the benefits of growing up on a farm. You learned to drive anything that had a motor

114

and wheels. Once again, competition was not lost on my brother and me. Whenever we got the opportunity, we would race the tractors on the road we lived on. Keep in mind, the road was a two-lane, winding, country road with exceptionally light traffic. We did occasionally experience the unexpected traveler, where one of us was expected to relinquish our lane to the oncoming car or truck. These occurrences usually resulted in the unsuspecting driver having to pull over because neither one of us would. Our grandparents received numerous reports of our mischievous behavior from the people that knew us and fortunately for us, there were no serious repercussions. You gotta love country life!

For a few years during my childhood, my uncle John was still living at home; and was more like a big brother to my brother, and me instead of an uncle. He was always in charge when my grandparents went shopping or to visit friends. We often had to bribe him to get to do things we all knew we were not supposed to. I would offer to starch and iron his shirt for his dates and my brother might offer to shine his shoes. These types of chores would be done in exchange for him allowing us to do something like setting up target practice. Yes, my grandfather had guns and while we knew they were off-limits, that did not prevent us from taking them out, setting up empty cans on a fence and taking our best shots. Sometimes we got away with not following through on our offer to complete tasks for my uncle because he would participate in the target practice too. We would remind him that he should not be using the guns and we could tell our grandparents if he told on us. Fun times. The same held true for my brother and I when we took my grandfather's and/or my grandmother's masonic regalia out of the wardrobe to play pretend—another off-limits activity. My grandfather was a Freemason, and my grandmother was an Eastern Star.

My uncle, John, blessed with a voice that would rival that of any of the well-known singers of that day or today, would sing in church on Sunday to please grandma, but secular music was his love. All three of us loved watching American Bandstand on Saturday afternoons and we often held our own version of it. My uncle would be the artist of the day and he would mimic artists like Jackie Wilson—including dropping to one knee or James Brown which included me or my brother assisting him with his cape. We were his audience and we constantly begged him to become a singer like the people he admired. He could have easily made it in the gospel music world or the secular music world—he had the voice and the writing skills—he was, and is, that great. When he sang at church, it was fun for him, particularly, when his performance resulted in the mothers of the church, ushers and church sisters shouting or running up and down the aisles of the church. You would never know, based on his performance, that he was not an earnest Christian at the time. Nothing happens before its time—today, he is a minister and started a gospel singing group, The *Zionnaires,* a few years ago.

I remember when he moved out and was no longer living with us. He was living in the same area and would come by often to help my grandfather with a task, have one of my grandmother's home-cooked meals or have me starch and iron his shirt. Things were not the same and we all missed him so much, especially my grandmother—she was incredibly sad about his leaving. I would hear her praying for him often. No matter if he was an adult, he was her child.

My grandparents raised my brother and me from infants and they did not have to. I am forever grateful for them. They gave us the best care they were equipped to provide.

We grew up without our biological mother and father. Oftentimes we look at our lives in comparison to the lives of others and think there is something missing; when really all we must do is appreciate the life we have and realize we are blessed beyond measure.

Yes, the work was hard, and the days were long; however, those years growing up on the farm helped to ground my uncle, my brother and me. Could our lives have been different, of course; but how different—better or worse? Do I wish I had grown up in the usual household—father, mother, and children—I used to wonder why I did not, but as I grew up, those thoughts faded. I remember all the childhood illnesses and who sat by my bed during those sleepless nights and who taught me how to cook, how to dress and carry myself and how to take care of a home. I remember who taught me how to drive, how to ride a horse bareback, how to shoot, who carried me to the bus in the mornings kicking and screaming, and who always challenged me and kept me on my toes in every contest. I am both thankful and grateful for my family.

All that I have accomplished would not have been possible without the upbringing and education I received in the rural community I call home. My grandparents drilled self-sufficiency in our heads. Both constantly reminded my uncle, my brother and me who we were (their child and grandchildren) and that we could do whatever we made up our minds to do. The womanhood education I received from my grandmother is invaluable. Those that knew her, knew that on Monday through Friday you may have mistaken her for just a hardworking farmer's wife; but come Sunday morning, when Sister Margaret Sutton stepped into Woods Grove FWB Church, she looked like she walked out of the Weil's store window. Often, I reflect on my life—two things happen—I smile, and I think of my grandmother and one of her favorite songs—*How I Got Over (*my soul looks back in wonder how I got over). I have had some struggles, disappointments and have fallen flat on my face a couple of times. The beauty in those falls was each time I fell, I got back up, brushed myself off and was better for it. I have had moments when I had to pinch myself to prove I was not dreaming—the accomplishments, the incredible experiences left me in awe. Those moments in my life were many and I refer to them as my God winked moments. I have worked for Fortune 500 companies, the U. S. Postal Service and for myself. Imagine a little shy, country tomboy owning her own business, practicing real estate for the past fifteen years while working full-time in the financial services industry, producing theatrical events, becoming a published author and an actor at sixty plus, making the Sixty over Sixty list (2018 in CT) and being named one of the One Hundred Women of Color (2020 in CT). All of us were raised to follow the example laid down for us by my grandparents—give to others when you can. I founded the *She Is Me Project* in 2014 and each year we purchase backpacks and school supplies for children in need. In 2021, we donated to five non-profit organizations, including Norwayne Alumni and Friends, Inc. I list these things not to boast but to demonstrate what God can do and how He will use you. I engage in many activities today; however, where I came from is what I wanted to focus on in this story. My greatest accomplishment to date is the role of mother to my son, Kejuan and G'Ma to my 15-month-old grandson, Miles.

Where you begin does not have to determine where you wind up. Some will say it's cliché but there truly is no place like home; and family are the people who care for you, nurture you and teach you the important lessons in life. Your foundation— family, community, church, school--is just like the foundation of a house—it supports you. I left North Carolina in 1972, after completing my sophomore year at Charles B. Aycock High School, for Connecticut. The only fond memories I have of the year at Charles B. Aycock are those involving some of my classmates. Prior to starting my first year at C. B. Aycock, my brother and I were at the corner store with my grandfather. As we were about to leave, three men were sitting on the steps in front of the store, and one asked my grandfather, "Frank, are you going to send them children to Aycock in the fall." My grandfather did not look back, kept walking to our car and responded; "well, I got a letter at the house telling me that is where they are supposed to go, so I reckon that is where they'll go." Another one of the three men said, "don't you think you might have some trouble if you do that?"? By this time, we were all inside the car and granddad started the car as he responded, "well, if I do have any trouble, I got something that hangs over my door that can take care of it"! My brother and I laughed so hard because we knew what granddad was referring to—his rifle. He kept a Remington hanging over he and my grandmother's bedroom door and a shotgun under their bed. The three men knew too because all their faces were crimson red as we drove away. Granddad was a no-nonsense kind of man and he feared no one.

Thankful does not seem sufficient to express how I feel about my heritage and my upbringing—it prepared me for the world I would face. Thankful and grateful for who taught me what I needed to know about womanhood, for who taught me I could do whatever I wanted to do, who taught me to sing—but could not give me the voice—dance and have fun, for who challenged me on every turn and always had my back 'til this day.

I want to impress upon the readers of this story, take pride in your heritage, your culture and embrace the richness of your foundation—your family, your community, and your school where you received your primary education. I have spent more years in Connecticut than I spent in North Carolina. Home for me is still Faro and Eureka, North Carolina, located in Wayne County—one of the one hundred counties in the Tar Heel State. I am and always will be a tar heel kid.

Break the Chains and Learn

My freshman year in high school has been one of my biggest challenges in life so far. It was a new experience for me socially and academically. I was diagnosed with autism when I was in the 2nd grade. I had an IEP throughout all my school years. I just needed a little help and staying focused on my work was really hard for me.

In high school my goal was to graduate with my diploma and not just a certificate. My least favorite subject and hardest subject was math. In my 10th grade year, a teacher told me that math was too hard for me, and I should just try to get a certificate and not continue with the higher-level math. I was determined to get a diploma like the rest of my family, so I opted to take the higher-level math. It was hard and I had to get a tutor, but I passed and graduated with my diploma. I was so proud of myself and was happy that I had made my parents very proud of me.

I was the quiet guy in high school from freshman to senior year and was always respectful to my teachers and fellow classmates. In high school I saw a lot of people bully others and make them miserable. I tried my best to not to be around troublemakers. My father always told my siblings and I to, "Be a leader, not a follower." In high school I was on the wrestling team for two years and decided not to return for my junior year so I could focus on my schoolwork. I also participated in the Christian Fellowship Club in high school where we did many activities, including praying for other students and staff. Completing high school with my diploma was a great accomplishment for me and motivated me to continue with my education and to accomplish more goals.

Wayne Community College

Year: 2020

After high school I attended Wayne Community College enrolling in Business Administration. At WCC I was involved in the Student Ambassador Program. The Student Ambassador Program provided opportunities to participate in campus activities, improve my public speaking skills as well as meet new people when assisting with tours of the campus. I also was a member and participated in the Future Leaders of America (FLOW) club. The FLOW club also allowed me to meet new people, participate in community projects and learn more about paths to take with a business degree. I also had the opportunity to attend the Men of Color National Summit, that was held at the University of Clemson in South Carolina for two years. This was a very memorable experience where we were able to meet and listen to successful Black men from all over the country talk about setting goals and how to be successful in life. The event included special guest celebrities from TV and radio shows. I even had a chance to meet and take a picture with Roland Martin, who was a special guest the first year I attended. Participating in the FLOW club was a very inspiring and motivating experience. Although some of my classes were challenging, I was able to get assistance when needed. I had to learn to focus and manage my time to study and get my work completed on time. My last semester at Wayne Community College was when COVID-19 made an impact. I had to change some things with my classes and was still able to graduate with a "B" average. I now have my Associates Degree in Business Administration.

My First Job

Year: 2020 – to Present

I started my first job working at Walmart right before Thanksgiving. I was hired as a seasonal temporary overnight stocker.

I had to get used to staying up and being on my feet all night. It was challenging at first, but once I finished training and learned how to do things I felt fine about my job. After the holidays were over, I was offered a full-time position which also came with a raise and a bonus. I have and am still learning and meeting new people. I still get a little nervous about meeting and talking to people I haven't met before although I am not as shy. Working at Walmart, I am also learning how to deal with different people and personalities. I am learning to not let negative people distract me or cause me to react in a negative way. I have plans to look for other jobs after I feel I have enough experience working at Walmart. My goal is to own a business one day and working at Walmart will provide the experience of customer service, teamwork, team building, work delegation, store appearance, product inventory, supervision, etc.

This is the end of my story and my advice to you is this. If you're going after your dreams, don't give up and keep moving forward. Stay in your own lane and try not to get involved with something that's going to hurt your chances of reaching your goals. Stay focused and ignore people that try to bring you down.

The last thing I want you to do is imagine yourself standing on a road, at the end of the road is your goal. Behind you is a giant rock and you're chained to it and cannot move forward. The rock represents negative people, mistakes, failures etc. And it's holding you back. If you want to reach your goal, break the chains and learn how to let go and ignore what is behind you and run to the goal you want to accomplish.

The Tree Speaks
(I Hear You Granddaddy)

Where the heck is that?" Then, I would say, "Have you ever heard of Pete Joyner's Gas and Grocery, perhaps, that sounds more familiar?" The tree that spoke to me stands tall, as if it is on guard, right in the middle of the landmark.

The store sat at the corner of, what is now, Lancaster Road and Big Daddy's Road. Yes, not far from *Dear Ole Norwayne School*. Some of you have confided in me, so, no I won't call names, that you used to skip school and go down to Pete Joyner's Gas and Grocery.

My Granddaddy was a short, fair-skinned gentleman. He welcomed all to his store and treated everybody the same. He probably lit up a cigar, sat back and enjoyed the conversations from these young stowaways. He loved to talk. My Grandmother, Lurenda, whom we called Mom Rendy, was a short, brown-skinned lady who loved to talk as well. Though she may have been a little more suspicious of these young students coming to the store during school hours, she most likely kept your little secret.

Granddaddy and Mom Rendy birthed one child, my mom, Ethel Mae. Ironically, she and my dad, Melvin Hobbs, married and had ten children. Granddaddy was quite overwhelmed when we came to visit. I must say, I don't think he really learned all of our names, so he called us all 'tots.' It didn't matter to me; all I know is that I loved my Granddaddy dearly.

I thought it was so cool that my grandparents ran a store. I was in candy and cookie heaven. Not only did they run a store, they lived there, too. They built living quarters in the back. The bedroom had knotty pine paneling. The kitchen was to the right, at the front of the store. I can remember the big wrought-iron bed with lots of old hand-stitched quilts piled on top. The dressers were made of heavy pine. I remember the vanity with a pine bench and a pink velvet cushion in the seat. There was an oval shaped black and white picture of them that hung on the wall, over their bed. A picture of the Lord's Supper hung on the wall in the kitchen. And yes, a picture of Jesus had its place on the wall in the bedroom as well. Mom Rendy had a porcelain white pitcher that sat in a basin on her vanity. She would threaten us if we got too close to it. That was her most prized possession. Oh yes, there was a velvet couch, an armchair, and rocking chair on one side of the room. That is where my sisters and I would sleep when we stayed over. They would only have two of us spend the night at a time. I managed to stay my fair share.

As much as I loved my grandparents, I am guilty of burying my happy childhood moments with them deep down into my subconscious, until one day I was driving by the landmark alone, and I heard a voice that said, "why didn't you slow down, or why didn't you stop, please don't forget me." You see, when my children were small, I used to slow down at this landmark and tell the story about my grandparents. After they grew up, I would tell the story to my grandchildren. Years went by and I did not pass that way. I have to ask myself if I was subconsciously avoiding this road. Needless to say, I was quite startled when I heard the voice. I looked in my rearview mirror and all that I saw was the tree. There it was standing alone in what is now a field. I'm thinking to myself, could this possibly be the same tree that stood beside my Granddaddy's store--the one we used to climb? I immediately stopped the car, got out, and said, "I hear you Granddaddy, I have not forgotten you." Yes, I know trees don't talk, right? It must have been the lock down from the Pandemic of 2020 that woke us all up. It was definitely a "time that tried men's souls." (Paine, Thomas, History)

The world seemed to have stopped. Perhaps, God was trying to get our attention. I don't know, but He got mine. Two Thousand

Twenty was a year of reflection, the good and the bad. It was the year of the murder of George Floyd, a 46-year-old Black man that drew national attention to Police brutality on Black People. The Black Lives Matter Movement was reborn. Our eyes were reopened to systemic social injustice on Black and Brown people. It drew something out of me that had been hidden for quite some time - the tragic loss of my Granddaddy. Memories of this tragedy emerged from my subconscious into my consciousness like a seedling that had been dormant until now.

It happened 53 years ago, when I was thirteen years old. I will never forget the loud shrill that my mom let out that day. My Mom was the nervous type. She squealed a lot. But there was something different about this time; it was a frightening sound. I could tell that something terrible just happened. The person on the other end of that phone said something to hurt her deeply. She didn't tell us what had happened right away. I remember her saying, "you all can't come with us." I heard my daddy talking about getting his gun, and he took the boys with him. I knew it was an urgent matter.

My heart was racing 100 bpm. My sisters and I stayed home not knowing what to expect when they came back. After what seemed an eternity, they finally came back. They brought my grandmother back with them, but where was Granddaddy? Why is Mom Rendy here and why is she crying? They gathered in front of us and told us what had happened. I thought I wanted to hear, but I did not want to hear any of it! I wasn't listening anymore! Not my Granddaddy! Somebody shot my Granddaddy! I was angry and scared at the same time. I did not know if they were coming to our house to get all of us or not. I was prepared to fight! They shot my beloved Granddaddy who was kind and never hurt anyone. Who would do such a thing and why?

The answer to that 'why' made me even angrier. Mom Rendy told us that a White man came into the store with his dog. The man asked my Granddaddy to give his dog some ice cream. He proceeded to putting his dog on the counter. This request may not sound so strange, but he wanted the dog to lick from the same tub that Grandaddy dipped for his customers. That's when my Granddaddy asked him to leave. They argued and the White man jerked the phone out of the wall, pulled out a pistol and shot my Granddaddy in the stomach. He was going to pull the trigger a second time, but Mom Rendy grabbed his arm and kept it up until he fired every bullet. I don't know where she got that strength, but had it not been for her heroic act, she would not have been alive to tell the story. I believe this man was on a mission. I am pretty sure he would have killed them both. He left, and a passerby came in to help my Grandparents, thank God!

Granddaddy did not die right away. He stayed in the hospital about twenty-two days before he succumbed to his gunshot wound to the stomach. That was the saddest day of my life. I would never hear him say, "come here tot, let me show you how to count money," or "you all can get a drink from the drink box." I often wonder how life would be if my Granddaddy had lived longer. I will never know, but I do know Pete Joyner's life mattered!

The tree spoke loud and clear that day. I don't know why the owner of that land spared it, but I am thankful they did. All these years, it stood as a reminder, a landmark of Pete Joyner's Gas and Grocery. I hear you Granddaddy, I hear you!

Jada Maliyah Williams   Charles B. Aycock Class of 2019

This is My Story

There are so many different people I know and meet daily, but only a few know the real, true, and valid story of Jada Maliyah Williams. As a child, I grew up with some health problems that required me to be sent to Wayne Memorial Hospital and other pediatric facilities. Even though I had these health conditions, I still was surrounded with love by God; my mom, Tracy Dawson; my grandmother, Mary Day; my aunt, Tamara Ray (aka Tammy); and more. Tracy Dawson has raised me all my life, and continues to be my rock, my heart, my number one supporter, and my life. Yes, I may have had a single parent, but my mom continued to display so much love that even two active parents' love could not compare to the love she has for me. I also had my aunt and my grandmother that not only expressed love but also brought so much silliness and laughter in my life.

When I started school at the age of five, I always put my schoolwork first. So, when I went to Charles B. Aycock High School, I wanted to make sure that I kept that hard-working mentality, so that when I started college, I'd have my focus on the right things. With that, when I decided to enter the AKA Miss 2019 Debutante pageant, I needed to learn more on how to balance school with my social life. During the entire debutante process, I had only missed one practice concerning school reasons. With everything I do, I make sure to put 100% of my attention into it, but if I feel I have too much on my plate or feel like I can't do something, I make sure to give it to God and pray about it. I read an article that once said, "With eliminating the word *can't* in your vocabulary, you will realize how many more opportunities you can create by removing that one word."

The night before I was crowned Miss Debutante, I had a dream that one of the other contestants won the crown and that I was first runner up. After the dream, I wasn't disappointed, but I knew if it did turn out the way it did in my dream, I would be so proud of myself for my work ethic and my ability to keep pushing when times went hard. Before I knew it, it was time to reveal the winner; and when my named was called for the Miss Francis J. Tyler Volunteer Award, Miss Scholarship, and Miss 2019 AKA Debutante Queen, I knew all my work had paid off and I also knew that I wouldn't have accomplished all I did receive that night without the help of God, my family, friends, church family, and small businesses in Fremont, Pikeville, and Goldsboro, North Carolina.

A few months after winning Miss Debutante, I was accepted to Campbell University with a scholarship. I started Campbell University as a nursing student, but then later during my spring semester of sophomore year I changed it to Kinesiology Physical Therapy. Since the change of majors, I have been happier than ever and knew that while in the midst of changing majors, I still desired to be in a field that continues to help others and change many people's lives. I'd never thought I would be "that student" to change majors during my college journey, but one thing I realized is that I wanted to be happy in the career that I was in. I didn't want to go to work and be unsatisfied with the career I chose. To any student or future college student reading this, do what makes you happy. If it gives you that drive to power throughout the day, you'll know if it's for you or not.

Now I am in my junior year at Campbell University and have already done so many things that impacted the Campbell University community. During the summer, I volunteered and served as a Tartan Leader (aka Orientation Leader) for the incoming class of 2025. My job and goal function was to guide the incoming students to different buildings around campus and for them to get the feel of what it is like being a student on campus. I was also supposed to be a role model for these students and teach them about the community at Campbell when it comes to Greek Life, Student-Life, the reason for Butler Chapel, the Student Union, etc. We consider ourselves family here at Campbell, so everyone, whether they are a Christian, have a different religion, or have no source of religion in their lives are welcome. As a campus, we do not discriminate and know that we have no right to judge others for their beliefs. If it weren't for being at Campbell University, I wouldn't be the headstrong, determined, and knowledge-based scholar I am today.

In life we have so many obstacles that we go through. At times, it feels like we are at our wits end, but we must remember and continue to remember that God does not put things on our shoulders that we cannot handle. So, if we continue to put God first and pray, we can inspire to be anything we want to be. That's how I have gotten this far, and that's how I am going to continue to live life after I graduate from Physical Therapy School. Never give it up because the universe is infinite and we as people can accomplish so much with the love of God and confidence.

Doris Worelds James-Taylor
Charles B. Aycock   Class of 1971

The Fly in A Glass of Buttermilk

With God's Blessing, I thank Him for my supportive mom, Julia Worelds Yelverton; my siblings, Morris, Jarvis, Linda and William; my husband James and, to Norwayne Alumni for giving me the chance to put my smothered thoughts to paper.

Approaching my 50th class reunion, I began to reminisce. I began to recall a time many, many years, but yet not so long ago.

It was in 1971. I was on Highway 117, and as I approached a billboard on my right, traveling between a little town called Pikeville to Goldsboro, North Carolina, I spotted a man on a horse. I've always admired horses. I remembered the beautiful sketches my brother Morris used to draw, like those of Trigger, Silver, My Friend Flicker and Penny's horse on Sky King. But the rider was not a cowboy like the shoot 'em ups, we loved to watch late nights on the old black-and-white TV. We had Gunsmoke, Rifleman, Lone Ranger, Roy Rogers, and Wyatt Earp. This man had on a long cape and to hide his face, not the mask like the Lone Ranger wore, but a white peaked Dunce cap on his head. And as we came closer to the billboard; and was about to pass it now, I read the caption across the bottom, that read: *Join the Klu Klux Klan, Sign up Today*. BOLD AS THAT! On a large billboard.

This was the atmosphere, and so I was not surprised, when the kids who were all up in our faces at school, pretended not to know us on Saturday's when they were downtown with their parents. I'd just say, that's OK. I know who not to bother with, next week, weeding out the good from the bad. Thank God for those, who were in fact, genuine.

Just so you know, the year before, my brother Morris and his classmates of 1970 were the last class to graduate from the *all Black school* of Norwayne. The next year, all schools were fully integrated, Norwayne School just happened to be the last. Charles B Aycock, the White school, became the High School, and Norwayne became the Elementary School.

So, the Class of 1971, my graduating class, was the first fully integrated class. With a ratio of 65% White/ 35% Black, my last year in high school was quite a transitional experience. When you've been uprooted and taken from a school where you have spent most of your life, it is quite a transition! For me, after eleven years in the same school system, the change fluttered with uncertain experiences. It did for most of us!

That school term, I called myself the FLY in a glass of buttermilk. I will attempt to show you just why:

- When too many of our talented Black athletes, not wanting to be just benchwarmers, refused to participate in sports rather than be omitted and overlooked by potential scouts...
- When the Principal, who never attended one single practice, chooses a White to be the captain of the Cheering Team and said, "You all didn't have football at your school, this is our first game. We need someone in charge to know what cheers to do, defensive or offensive. We'll let one of you all lead the second half," but he does not...
- When you're NEVER called to the guidance counselor's office to even discuss your qualifications or possibilities of any financial assistance or further education...
- When 37 out of the 56 seniors who did not even want to take their graduation pictures for the yearbook were Black...
- When you realize that any 'ole excuse would do to keep us in the background...

I became that FLY in that glass of buttermilk because I was determined that we were not going to be pushed under the rug, overlooked, ignored nor second in line. ALWAYS? No, *NOT* all of us! If I had to be the only one present, that FLY in a glass of buttermilk, then so be it!

When you are a FLY in a glass of buttermilk, how do you respond? Can you imagine that? My situation? How I felt? How it looked? Picture the image; disrupting the usual pure white calm...the struggle, just to stay afloat...with soaked wings, it is almost impossible to fly. Now picture what the owner of the glass of buttermilk felt. You know how it feels. I was the intruder, the defiler, messing up some anticipated pleasure, I was the contaminator! I'm sure there was some disgust! Oh, well.

If I had to be that FLY in that glass of buttermilk, then so be it indeed! This was my major motivation. That year, I got into everything I could. Driven to, if nothing but to be a speck in every eye, become obviously visible. If I were the only distraction, I was determined we would not be excluded! My single, major motivation, I had to "represent" our existence, and not be omitted.

Going through my CBA yearbook, Class of '71, surprisedly, my FLY mentality achieved: Library Aid Award; Office Aid Award Student Government; National Honor Society; Monogram Club; Co-Head Cheerleader Captain; Homecoming Court Rep; Semi-Finalist in the Miss Aycock Pageant (I was told by another White contestant's mom, that I should have won; voted Most Talented instead); Member of the Chorus Glee Club; Top Salesman, (could sell ice to an Eskimo; French I Award; McNerney Leadership Award and received a $100 Scholarship as Debutante for the AKA Sorority.

I venture to say, I do not believe it was because I was that good, but because I was that visible. I'm sure when they had to choose a Black *AND* a White, for whatever campaigns and position going on, they didn't know my name, but they saw my face and probably asked, "Who was that Colored girl (FLY) in this or that?

Mom told me much later, she was so glad I finally graduated, without ever complaining once, that she was taking me everywhere I needed to go, to celebrate all that I participated in. Love you, Mom!

Today, this FLY mentality has shaped my life with strong faith, to become a top recruiter in my own Home-Based Business, to earn a play name of Bulldog, and to own a trademark for my clergy fashion designs. I am retired but thanks to my God, I ain't finished yet! This FLY finally got free and has excelled because of it! And because there were obviously others who stayed on the path, pressed forward in our attempts to fit in, feel included, have our suggestions considered and not feel like strangers in a barren land. I was pleasantly proud to see in the pictures posted on Facebook of Charles B Aycock's 50th Class reunion, some of the efforts we attempted to make a change in 1971, came to pass: adding Norwayne's GOLD (from their Royal Blue & Gold) to Aycock's BLUE (Carolina Blue and White); and the Ascot became the GOLDEN Falcons! Hats off to those students and teachers, who followed in our footsteps, paving the way, accomplishing from what I see… a cultural BLEND! I believe that we, the class of '71, were truly chosen, by God, to break that ground, tread the paths, be the trailblazers.

God, we thank you, even 50 years later, for those who still seek equality! Times and hearts are changing for some, the others are just 50 years older. With Your help and guidance, we'll see gray, instead of black or white; compromise, instead of right or wrong.

From life to death, what we do with that dash in the middle that He gave us, we need to make it count.

Free to FLY.

40 Years and Welcome Back Home

Preface

I will start out by saying…I have not opened a business, become an actor, authored any books, joined a sorority, or made a public name for myself. I am not a millionaire yet, but I am a Lifetime Member of Norwayne Alumni and Friends Inc. and a child of GOD! I have always known since the age of three that God's angels watch over me. My assigned Angel's name is Gabriel. I have seen him and felt his presence; he has come to my rescue many times before. You will see his name throughout my story. God is probably saying, "Really, what do you want Me to fix now? You can do it yourself!" God does have a sense of humor.

What you will read in my story is just a snapshot of some experiences in my life. I do not expect some of you to understand what I am writing about or even agree with what I have to say, but this is my story and a part of my life I decided to share, which may one day become a book with more details.

How have I survived? I am a warrior, who learned to live life with the cards I have been given. Laugh at the trials and tribulations although it is hard when going through it. But when you get through it, laugh until your side hurts and tears come rolling down your eyes. Seeing the good in your trials and tribulations will help you to get over it and it will no longer hurt and can help you to be at peace with things. Find someone to always love, even if it is only God at times, for humans will fail you, but God never will.

The wonderful thing I found is I can talk to God anywhere and anytime. I know my God given name and I know he is always willing to listen. God knew these trials and tribulations would happen before I did. Sometimes it is his way of getting your attention when you need to be drawn nearer to Him.

We all have a life story, some of us like to speak about our accomplishments and some of us prefer not. I decided to share what I know is real. At this stage of my life, I can honestly say living in today's world is not easy. I have trotted paths that I had no idea I would travel or where that path would take me. However, my theory has been, "Whatever it is, it is, deal with whatever life throws your way, and live the life you've been given!" God knew this before I entered my mother's womb. God had a plan for my life from the very beginning. I used to think I had control of my life; traveling these paths to get me where He wanted me to be. Until my days on earth are done, He is in control and has been in control all along. Even when I have steered away from the things I should have done. Even through trials and tribulations, broken and a few bruises, I am still standing. I can see clearly now, and I am still standing.

I always wonder just exactly what my God gifted talent was, my mother told me that all of God's children have an assigned gift. I started eliminating the things I could do with ease and the ones I was good at. God's gift I felt was something you do with ease, where others had to learn how to do it. I tried my hands at singing and realized I can sing just a little bit but not that well. I wanted to play the piano, even taught myself to play a few songs and realized that is not it. So just exactly what is it? I watched my mother sew for years and when she sat down at the sewing machine, she was so happy. She would sew and sing and was good at designing clothes. She even made a living sewing every day and never was there a day that she did not enjoy sewing until...the day my father passed away. Mother never really sewed much again. It was as if that day took her joy away. My mother taught me how to sew, but I did not enjoy it. I realized quickly that it was her God given talent and not mine. So, after years of wondering just what it is that I do with so much ease, after so many people told me I seemed to always know how to express myself and when to say it. Then, I realized it's more to my gift than words. It is something I have had from the very beginning of my life. If you continue reading my story, you will discover what God has given me.

I dedicate this story in loving memory of my mother and father. My mother 's favorite phrase was "SAY WHAT," in her southern twang accent. Whenever I hear someone say those words, I feel as if she is speaking to me and just chuckle.

I was born a preemie, only weighing 3lbs. Back in the 50's, the survival rate for a 3lb baby was not something that normally happened. I was the only child of my mother to be born in a hospital. Surviving my siblings was more trouble than being born prematurely. My mother said I cried a lot and my brother and sister hated me and all the noise (kids just don't understand and they wanted my mother to take the crying baby back to the hospital, but I continued to grow and become strong, but was often sick, so what I'm going to say next may make you wonder as it often makes me wonder, do I remember this or is it the story my mother told me that I remember? I have always had a very sharp memory, but for some reason it seemed too real. I was about the age of two, I was crawling on the floor, the reason I to this day say I remember it, because I can tell you exactly where the bottle was located. Back in those days we had wood heaters to keep us warm, my father would feed it wood all day and night, my father had left a bottle of kerosene in a Pepsi bottle on the right side of the wood heater this is why I say I remember it because I can remember exactly where it was located, he used this to restart the fire in the pot belly stove when it would go out. Even as a child, I loved Pepsi. As a child, I saw a bottle, so I crawled to it. Well, we had a bottle laying around and I opened the bottle and turned it up. Little do I know, in the bottle was kerosene. According to my mother, I immediately went into a seizure. Then, she realized I had swallowed kerosene because the smell was on my breath, and I had to be rushed to the Doctor's office.

Back then, the doctor's office was segregated with two signs that read White or Colored. You know, I was supposed to go to the Colored line, but that day my mother was told to take me to the White line to be seen right away. After being seen by the doctor, he informed my mother that I would not make it through the night, but I am still here. Living life, in the 21ˢᵗ century. My mother took me home. She prayed and prepared herself for the worst. A baby bird flew in the house and circled the room. Beliefs from those days were, if a bird came into your house, it was a sure sign that death was near. My mother wrapped me in her bed and as night drew near my temperature continued to rise in the 100, 102, 103, and 104. As perspiration covered my body, she continued to pray, and I fell asleep. Then suddenly out of nowhere, I woke up and sang the words to this song, "All Day and All Night the Angels Watch Over Me." Again, I immediately went off to sleep. My mother said she thought she had lost me, but the next morning I woke, fever gone and memory fine (Thanks Gabriel).

I tell this portion because it was the beginning of what my God's gift was for me but did not realize it until I reflected on my life and put all the pieces together. Remembering the words from my mother, which I did not understand at the time, I always listen to her speak God's words but not dwelling on her words until an exceptionally long time. Finally, I accepted the fact that I am really a special child of God. I have a special gift that God gave me. I thought everyone could do what I do, or see what I can see, but came to grips with only what I have. This gift is just for me.

My life's special gift shines through again. When I was 4 years old, Hurricane Hazel hit the North Carolina (NC) shore on October 15, 1954. It was one of the deadliest in NC history killing 469 people with winds at 130 miles per hour. I remember this hurricane and sitting on the floor in my parent's room with my siblings in an old wooden house. We heard the wind howling and rain falling. We saw trees and debris flying everywhere. After the hurricane passed over, my father felt it was safe for him to go out to check the damages and go to the neighborhood store. Suddenly on his way back home to us, the eye of the hurricane came back bringing more devastating winds, rains, and damages. Stronger than the first hit of the hurricane, my father could see the house as he tried to walk home. The winds were so strong, he could no longer walk or stand up. So, he began to crawl and as he pressed onward, suddenly, he looked up and saw the winds take the roof off the house we were in. My mother realized she had to protect her children and told us to hold onto each other because we had to flee the house. The house was falling on top of us. Mother took us out to the back of the house where there was an old kitchen that had no windows. The old one was detached from the house as we dodged bricks and debris to get there. Once we got inside this old kitchen, the wind went through it, but we were safe. Even still, we were afraid. Clinging together and shivering from the chilly rain but somehow, we felt safer than staying near the house. As the winds and rain continued, I stated to my mother that I heard my father. She said no, your father went to the store. I said, I know, but mommy, I heard my father calling for us, and yes, I was correct. (Gabriel) While he was crawling in the ditch, two White soldiers were riding in their jeep, surveying damages and saw my father. They stopped to help him. He informed them; his family was in that house that you just saw the roof missing. They immediately stepped on the gas and assisted him getting to us. They tried to get through the front door that was still standing with wood and bricks still falling. Once my mother finally listened to me (Gabriel), she heard what I was talking about, she grabbed us, and we tried to go where my father was located. We met them in the hallway. My father and the soldiers tried to take us around the side of the house but realized it was much too dangerous. So, we ended up going back through the falling house to get to the front door. My father, mother, siblings, and I along with the two soldiers got into their Jeep. They took us safely to my grandfather's house about a half of a mile down the road. This was a trial and tribulation of survival and God's grace and mercy.

Remembering Grammar School, at Eureka, I loved and enjoyed school. I never wanted to miss a day from first grade. I even contracted chicken pox and had my mother take me to school just for roll call, so I could be counted present and not miss a day. My biggest concern daily was being able to get chocolate milk, never liking milk at all even as a baby. However, I did like the chocolate milk, but for some reason they only gave each class a certain amount, so I had to have my mother tell the teacher I would throw up the white milk and please give me the chocolate. After several mishaps, I finally got to get the milk I liked to drink. Whenever I had any controversial moments with any of my teachers, I would always let my father know. Once I informed my teacher, if she tried to spank me or continue giving me a tough time, I was going to tell my father and he would come to school and punch her in her big stomach (chuckling). By now, you should realize I was a daddy's girl at an early age.

When I moved on to third grade my first year of Norwayne School, I felt we had moved on up to the Eastside (like the Jefferson). School was so much fun. As the years passed, grade third through eighth went quickly. Before I knew it, I was in Junior High. I was normally quiet unless someone bullied me, and I would fight back with not even rationalizing the situation. Genuinely, I enjoyed ninth grade, cheerleading, being a member of Glee Club and participating in any school plays, dances, and contests. I remember one of the most beautiful contests the school had, was a Hula Hoop contest. Seeing all the kids on the gym floor and every color of the rainbow of hula hoops. I even remember a student from Class 1965 was the winner because he could hula hoop from his neck to his arms, legs, and hips all at the same time. The basketball games, graduations, musical concerts, and plays were all my favorite. My most memorable times of school were short lived, and I did not see it coming.

At the end of the school year of 1965 became the beginning of desegregation of schools in North Carolina. Letters were mailed out to all parents. It read: If you want your child to attend Charles B.

Aycock, please sign and submit your child's name. Well here again, surviving my siblings came into play again. My sister who just graduated in 1965 and was going off to college convinced my mother that she should send me. By using this fact, I would be getting a better education. "Excuse me, I am over here." But no one asked me or considered my opinion on the matter. Not one soul even considered or gave second thought of what I might have to endure. It did not matter because come September after Labor Day weekend I was off to the all-White (at that time) high school.

I was never nervous behind any of it. Angry was more the word. From day one, I convinced myself you can do this, my father had already taught me how to fight, how to shoot soda cans off a stump with a double-barreled shotgun, reload and brace yourself because it's going to kick, drive a car like a race car driver to get away from anyone trying to follow me or run me off the road. I was ready but, not having a clue what to expect.

My mother was a seamstress and always made sure I was impeccably dressed. I had a dress for every day of the week. It was the first day of school. Well, here I go. All dressed up in my Sunday's best and waiting on the porch for the bus because my mother enrolled me at Charles B Aycock. Given a timeframe as to when the bus would pick me up, I remember my father being in the front yard that morning as to say to those on the bus, you better not lay a hand on her. When the bus stopped, I stepped on and my father said, "I'll see you this afternoon." As I climbed the steps of the bus and started to go for a seat, some of the White kids started calling me Nigger, bad names, and playing musical chairs. So, I would not be able to get a seat, I will never forget these words. "I thought you all said we were getting niggers on our bus, she isn't no nigger," then another one said, "yes, she is. Just because she is light, she is still a Nigger!" Then finally, the bus driver told them to shut up and move out of the seat to let me sit down. Otherwise, I was determined I am going to stand right here all the way to school and dare you to touch me. I still remember the first day when most White kids saw all the other Black people down the hall at school, they would scream and climb the walls to get away from us. Like we were wild animals from the jungle of Africa.

The afternoon on the ride home, I listened to some of the White kids say, "Well she is a Nigger, because I saw all assorted colors of them today, but this one has freckles." The other one said, "I don't care she is still a nigger." Yes, my father was waiting for me when the bus stopped at our house and before I could walk in front of the bus to get across the highway, he said, "Are you okay?" For 3 years, I was the only Black person on my bus ride coming and going to school. I traveled the roads alone every single day. Am I a loner? Where is my help? Well, I had to tread this path alone. Oh, how can I forget? Gabriel was always with me.

The mentality from some of the White kids went on for three long, long, years. I hated Monday mornings, and looked forward to Friday afternoons every single school week. I can only remember the principal's name, my Algebra, French, and Typing teachers. The rest of my school days are a blur because I blocked them out of my memory. I was an A student at Norwayne but at Aycock, I only did what was necessary to graduate each year. Something I once loved, going to school became something I hated, I mean hated on a day-to-day basis. There was no NAACP checking on us, no counselors, no teachers, or principals that seemed to care. Every day at school, I learned to be present but not present. I daydreamed all the time, looking out the windows at school and taking my mind away from it all. I dreamt of walking the streets of Paris, France. The only class I enjoyed was typing. While typing, I let my fingers do the walking and learned to put rhythm to it so that when I got my first government job from my typing skills, people would stand in the hallway just to listen to the sound of the rhythm from my typewriter. I enjoyed French class because again it connected me to France, and I would try my best to imitate the recordings of the language and accent as we practiced speaking through our daily drills.

I never heard from my old friends at Norwayne, saw some of them at church, but no conversation. Gone were the school activities I so once loved. Gone were my friends I once had. Then, I came to realize, it is a do or die, and you are on your own. Never a day went by that the bus ride home was not a miserable ride. At night sometimes, we received death threats, with words like, "We going to kill you, bomb your mailbox or burn a cross in your yard."

Of course, my father and I were always ready and waiting to protect ourselves. For three long years this lasted but I was determined to look out for myself and my cousin, fight if I had to and fight, I did. When you finally say, you have had enough and enough is enough. One day some of the kids started throwing spitballs. For those not knowing what that is, spit on paper, roll it up in a ball and throw it, and depending upon the size it can cause harm. I immediately stated, loud and clear to all sitting behind me. "This is your last warning, whoever is throwing the spitballs at me, better stop, for if the next one hits me, you'll be sorry." They continued, so I got up out of my seat, went to sit in the seat behind mine; and the kids sitting there immediately threw up their hands to keep from getting hit and said it was not me. So, I went to the next seat and grabbed the first person I saw and started swinging. You would think I would have stopped to think, you are the only Black child on this bus, they could jump you and beat you, but I was angry. I did not care. The Bus driver slammed on the brakes and stopped the bus. He said, "what's going on? You better leave her alone." Little did I know, we were close to my house and as usual when I am in trouble my father and Gabriel always knew it and were ready to come to my rescue. He saw the bus stop at the top of the hill and immediately knew something was wrong. By the time the bus got to my house, my father was already on the side of the road waiting for me to see what happened. When I stepped off the bus, he said what happened and before I could finish telling him, like in one of Madea' s movies, where she stated, "I'll see you at 3 o'clock," My father was on that bus. He told the bus driver if anyone lay a hand on her I will come for you. After that incident, I did not have any more trouble and every day I felt special because I always had a seat waiting for me and not a soul said or threw anything at me again. Near the end of my last year, my father let me drive to school every day and it relieved some of my stressful days.

My experience at Charles B. Aycock made me make the decision, if I ever got away from North Carolina, I never ever planned to return. Ending my tenure there and off to college I went, leaving college after a year, I headed further north from Wayne County and North Carolina.

Currently, I am not going to discuss my life for 40 years, but during the 40 years being away, I continue to realize my special gift. That wonderful father of mine departed this earth way before I was ready for him to go, but God wanted him and even on his deathbed, he was still showing me things. At the end, he showed me how to accept death. Gone too soon. He always said, "I never worry about you, you are strong and prepared, you will be fine." A month before his death, as sick as he was, he got out of his recliner and got down on the floor with my only grandson, while he had yet begun to walk and had a mind-to-mind talk with him. Shortly after, my grandson at 10 months of age took his first steps and till this day whatever they discussed during their floor meeting, my grandson has the mindset of a person much older than his age, so I inform him often that my father left him his wisdom, when their minds met. My grandson is often few of words, like my father, but always analyzing every thought.

After my father's death, my mother became lost without him. For their ladder years of their life together, he treated her like royalty and her favorite words were, Say What, and to God Be the Glory. It was not three months after my dad's death that again my special gift kicked in (Gabriel) and I realized that my mother was simply going through the motions. She was with people and did the things they always did together, but she was not present. Once I realized something was wrong, other than being afraid to live alone, I knew we had to make some changes for her well-being. Ask yourself, how do you oversee your elderly parent whose lifestyle is about to change? The elderly love to hang on to their independence and will fight to the very end. They think they are capable of caring for themselves and doing the things they always did without your help. They feel you are trying to take everything away from them and you are treating them like a child. When you are their child, and the roles begin to reverse, often the mind says, "I can but the body says no, you can't." So, where do you go from here?

The questions we often ask. When did it begin? Why does it happen? Can dementia be reversed? What age does it begin? The medical field only knows one thing for sure, it has not, as to date, found to be reversible. It only gets worse as time passes by and it affects everyone differently. While most of the symptoms remain the same in most people, each person's personality plays a big part in their everyday life. Dementia puts most of its stress on the caregiver, more than the person that has the disease. When a dementia person has something on their mind, thoughts are planted in their mind and you could try to get them to change that thought until you turn blue in the face and they will not change their thought, because in their mind they are correct. The caregiver is thinking for two, their patients and themselves, while still trying to keep their patience as calm as possible.

My mom's dementia was led on by first, stress and anxiety attacks that happened in her life. My mother, being one of the Godliest women I know, had an aneurysm. A blood vessel leaked in her brain one Sunday morning while she was at church, singing in the choir and suddenly, appeared one of her sisters whom she had not seen for a while and had some disagreements with walked into church. Shortly after seeing her sister, my mother was standing up singing and simply fell to the floor. At first my father thought that she had gotten filled with the Holy Spirit and Holy Ghost and fell on the floor, but quickly realized that was not the case. My father rushed her to the hospital and when she was x-rayed it was found she had

144

blood leaking from her brain and was medevacked to Greenville Hospital; this hospital was equipped to manage her condition. When my sister and I arrived, she knew my sister but not me and the doctor's told us that they would be preparing her for brain surgery the next morning because the medication given was not stopping the leakage. My family was blessed, the doctor said, that it leaked and not burst. My mother truly lived a life to live again and always praised and gave God all the glory. The next morning, just before taking her down for surgery, the hospital did another brain scan and there was no leakage. It simply sealed itself and no surgery was necessary, and she was soon released from the hospital. However, the doctor informed her, a miracle happened, one that they had not seen before and advised my mother she would need to take medication for her brain for the rest of her life. My mother did not want to hear that or believe it because she knew God had truly healed her and that was all she needed. Yes, God is real. He has all powers to heal, but God gave man the brains to help us along, and he helps those that help themselves. However, there was no convincing my mother of this, she stood firm and refused any additional medication and stood on God's promises. My mother did all right physically for a longtime, but when my father died, so much of her died with him. He was a wonderful father and became a wonderful husband when he found God one day. Wherever and whenever you saw him, you saw her. While she enjoyed her God given talent in sewing, my father took care of everything else, even cooking, shopping, and keeping the house in order. His love was his yard as if they became one. The day my father died she informed my sister and me that my father told her something, but by that time his voice had become weak and soft. My mother had a hearing problem, so she never got to understand or hear exactly or clearly what he had to say. That was the very beginning of her dementia, because in her mind, she kept trying to figure out what he was saying to her, and no matter how hard she thought about it, she could not produce the answer. She wouldn't let it go, many, many years later she would often say, I still wonder what your father was trying to tell me.

My father did give my mother a request before he died, but she did not honor his request and when I often wonder why she did not listen to him, I finally concluded, because of her motherly love that perhaps went further than some mother's love. Sometimes I feel that we do need tough love, love with your mind and your heart, sometimes that love can tear you apart and destroy your well-being. We often feel and ask God to handle things, but we will not totally let go, and allow God to fix it. We don't want to take our hands off it. If you know, God has it, God is going to fix it, then we must have tough love and let him fix it, he truly will fix it. May not be the way we want it to be fixed, but as the song says, Jesus Will Fix It After A While.

My mother being under the watchful eye of my brother for years, one day I was at work doing inventory and standing up against the wall, thoughts came to mind, call your mother. As normal I ignored it but it kept pressing on my mind, call your mother, I realize that special gift I have wouldn't let me turn away from it (Gabriel). I called and found she was in desperate need of help. She had become quiet and disoriented and needed to go to the hospital. I contacted her neighbor, asked her to remain with her until I could get her brother over, she was home alone. I informed my uncle and told him I would call him back in 30 minutes. He could look at her disposition and assess her medical needs. When I called back, he informed me she needed further medical assistance. Well, granted, I am a five-hour drive away, it is snowing and sleeting. My sister is out of the country, and I am unable to locate my brother, again my father's training and Gabriel came to play. I immediately contacted my supervisor and stated, "I must go." I never went home; I contacted my daughter, informed her of the situation, asked her to pack my clothes, come to my job, bring me the other car and I am on the road. It was about eight o'clock pm. I left with only one thought, I have to make it to

146

her, popped in my favorite Fleming Sisters CD, my road music, and headed south. Before I could get to Richmond the snow was falling heavily and the roads were becoming icy, and I was crossing patches of ice and my car was sliding. I remember my father's words, "if you are traveling on the road and you run into trouble and you need help, get behind a long-distance truck, blink your lights a certain number of times, that will let them know you need help or stop at a truck stop and let them know." Continuing, I followed his instructions and the truck in front of me paved the roads all the way until I reached Wilson. I blinked my lights to say thanks and made my turn. Thank God and my angel (Gabriel) otherwise my mother may have been awarded to the custody of the state, because she was left alone too long. When finally released from the hospital, my mother went to live with my sister for her dementia was at a different stage.

Dementia Symptoms

1. Always looking trying to find something for hours, it is there most of the time, but they do not recognize that is what they are looking for.

2. Going places, driving in a car and starting to forget how to get home.

3. Constantly paying bills, the same one repeatedly.

4. Wearing the same clothes, repeatedly for days in a row.

5. Repeating the same conversation, repeatedly and not remembering they already told you 10 times or more already.

6. No interest in the things they used to do or not wanting to do the things they always did.

7. The far-away stare, not remembering what day or time it is, or what year it is.

8. Hearing a phone ring but not answering it or forgetting to hang it up.

9. Clutter begins with stacking things everywhere and anywhere, always searching for things but cannot remember what they are looking for.

10. Putting things in odd places, like keys in the refrigerator, hats in a microwave.

11. Not sleeping, sleepwalking all night, or working on projects all night long, never relaxing or resting.

12. Knowing they are losing their memory but fighting with anyone trying to help them for they try to hang onto their independence and do not need your help. The symptoms go on and on.

13. Dementia is such a tricky disease, you must spend time with that person to notice their behavior changes, sometimes they are present with you and next moment they are not, they are in a world of unknown but have half of their mind with you and the other half in their world. It is much more comforting to them when you go into their world and not try to convince them that what they are saying and doing is wrong. They don't see it that way. Caregivers sometimes try to set them straight on the right answer, but they are convinced their thoughts are correct.

You cannot change the dementia mind, you are wasting your time trying to correct them, you only frustrate yourself and they often become angry with you, and you become their enemy, while some become violent, combative, and hard to manage.

Find the humor in it, because they often do and say funny things; even God has a sense of humor. It is the best way to get through it, trying to figure out the why is and why not is impossible, they are stuck and will not change. While dementia is so tricky at times, most people can cover up this disease at times, their conversation is on point, and you think they are doing good and within a blink of the eye they have flipped the switch. You must spend time with the person in the beginning of dementia to detect something is wrong, but the most important sign is repeating, they start to repeat the things they say and do, repeatedly and yet they still are able to do normal functions until one day they do not anymore. Each person may show different signs, there are four stages that some go through, the old saying, once an adult, twice a child, belongs to dementia patients. It's an adult that starts to reverse its life cycle, they leave adulthood, become a teenager in mind again, then a child with childlike behavior, to the final stage, a baby. However not everyone goes through all the stages, the ones that do, it's a hard battle for they know they are losing their independence, and they fight until the very end to remain a well minded adult.

After my mother spent several years under my sister's care, the desire to return to her own home never left her and she would ask my sister daily, when are you going to take me home? My sister always told her, when you allow me to take you there, realize you can't stay there by yourself and be willing to return with me without a fight, I'll take you. I always promised my mother that when I retire, I would take her back home to stay. Well retirement came earlier than I anticipated. I picked up my mother from my sister and drove her home, while a tornado landed just behind us. We drove through the high winds and rain with my granddaughter in tow in the front seat begging me to stop, while my mother never batted an eye and just kept asking me if I was seeing all right, until we reached her doorstep (Gabriel.) She did not want to stop until she got home. When we reached her house, even though she was having trouble walking, she immediately got out of the car as if she had never had surgery. She had taken a bad fall and broken her hip. She walked straight to her bedroom, remembering where everything was and said, "Thank you Jesus."

Now, the title of my story reads, *40 Years and Welcome Back Home.* My mom longing to go home, even with dementia, brought me home.

Was I ready to come back? Absolutely not, for I had to leave my family who had been together since the birth of my children and

149

grandchildren, but I knew I had to honor my promise to my mother. I knew her days were winding down and if I did not, I would regret it the rest of my life. I always was taught to honor your mother and father and your days would be lengthened upon this earth. I had no choice but to honor my promise and grant my mother her fondest wish.

Like off to desegregate the schools of North Carolina, I had no clue on how I was going to do this alone. A house to take care of, a car, a strange place I never lived in, no job, living in a place I only visited and did not remember a lot about where places were in NC. Forty years had passed, things had changed and even though I visited frequently, I didn't really go places except to church and my mother's and father's house. Again, I had to convince myself you got this, you can do this, but alone with an elderly dementia mother, to God I prayed daily for help. I missed my home, I missed my family, I missed my friends and where in the heck were the streetlights. It is dark here; you cannot see your feet or hands outside at night and my mother's house was near the woods. I knew some of the neighbors but not all of them and they were getting older and sick as well. You know, it is too quiet here. I heard crickets and frogs at night, and oh, there goes a fox in the woods, as well as raccoons and snakes. What else is in those woods and the thoughts would go on and on through my mind. Until again, I had to convince myself you got this. I could always count on my cousin, the one I always helped protect in school. She and her husband would help look out for me and I finally convinced myself, child, just pray and go to bed, you got this too. You remember, now, I lay me down to sleep. I pray to God my soul he keeps, if I should die before I awake, I pray to God to keep me at peace. God and my Angel Gabriel watches over me every night. These were my praying words. As time went by within the two-year period of taking care of my mother, physically healthy but a quiet dementia mind, I saw her start to decline. The day came when she could no longer walk or stand up. I knew I would need some additional help from someone, and I reached out to her doctor and the Department of Aging for help. Both assisted me in providing additional home care. All the aids were excellent caregivers and most of the time I had someone for three or four hours, Monday through Friday.

Weekends I was on my own and sometimes when aides were unable to come, I had to do it all alone. When my mother became unable to move on her own, I had to learn to use a lift to get her in and out of bed. I refused to just let her stay in bed all day, so I got her bathed, dressed, fed, lifted her, and put her in her recliner so she was able to sit up and watch people come and go and look out the door. I was her caregiver twenty-four hours a day. The aids came early and by midday they were gone. The majority of the time, I only had an hour of time to get out to get fresh air, do grocery shopping or run errands. Again, I kept reminding myself, you got this.

As I watched my mother become a baby all over again, there was one thing she never forgot and that was God. As I said daily prayers to her, read scripture, sang to her, she always let me know that she heard me, when she would no longer talk. And oh, that gift I always wanted to be able to play the piano, I would get on the piano and play one of the songs I learned to play, "Yes, God is Real." Her eyes would light up and she would pat her feet. Now you do know I am positive I was not playing it correctly, but it sounded good to me and her at the time. The second gift I tried to do, I would sing to her and oh when I hit the high notes, she would look at me as if to say, "you go girl." Mother never forgot anything that was Godly. Before she stopped talking, she would sing all the church hymns with me out of her song book and go through all the songs I remembered from my childhood. So again, they often hold onto what they love. I would often see my mother looking in the corner to the east of any room she was in. I would ask her, "who is it that you see?" I could tell from the look on her face, she saw someone, and she would say, she saw her mother and father. I honestly believed she did for they were beckoning her to come on home to her final resting place.

My mother genuinely loved God and stood by his every word, all the way till the end and never stopped giving him praise.

Getting close to the end of my story, I will say, be ever so careful what you choose to cherish in life, for none of us know where life will take us, whose hands we may fall in, or when our time will come, try to never say never. Forty years ago, I said the word never. I never, ever planned to return to North Carolina but through all I went through, God sent me back because of my mother and His Grace and Mercy upon her. To God Be the Glory, (her favorite words.) SAY WHAT? SAY WHAT?

While taking care of my mother every year during Labor Day weekend, I would attend the Norwayne Alumni banquet event and functions. My daughter would take care of my mother so my sister and I could attend the weekend festivities. I attended the parades and banquets. I enjoyed seeing my former classmates, but never got to stay to connect with others, I had to get back to my mother. After my mother's death, I relocated to another area. After years of encouragement from my classmate, who took the place of keeping my father's lawn the way he did, and my BFF, who kept encouraging me to come join, and put a wall plaque in your parents' name, I decided to continue to participate in the affairs. When it was our Class 50th reunion, I finally decided to become an active member with my classmates. We worked on fundraiser projects, and suggested changes to help enhance the Norwayne Alumni Association. Some of the changes we suggested have made a significant impact on the association, due to the fact that the President and Vice President were willing to listen and try our ideas. I became involved in the Food Bank donations, yearly class donations, and soliciting donations from companies and family members. I will say, had it not been for my mother bringing me home, I do not think I would have become as involved with the organization. I started selling raffle tickets by text messages, emails, and phone calls to my friends, my daughter's friends, and my family members. Along came COVID-19, and since the way I sold the raffle tickets worked for me, I once again used that technique to solicit family members for further donations, since we were not able to have a banquet weekend. It began with my aunts getting wall plaques and getting one in honor of my parents. My aunts gave class donations as well. After they received personal thank you notes from Norwayne Alumni President, they decided to continue to give, for my aunt stated she always give to her church and other charitable organizations, not always knowing for sure what her donations were being applied to, she rather give more to the Norwayne Alumni for she can see the good the organization is doing in helping people and to receive a response from her donations meant a lot to her. My aunts' daughters became involved as well in support of their parents and gave additional donations. Both of my aunts became Lifetime members and yearly class donors. I became a lifetime member to support my aunts. Then the thought came to me to make the donations a family affair and contacted all the children of my father's siblings, since only two are living and the rest are deceased, but all his siblings attended Pikeville Training School or Fremont. He had one brother, his nephew gave a donation in honor of his father, three of his sister's children gave donations in honor of their mother. I named these donations the Yelverton Klan and credited my endeavors to the Class of 1968. These donations have become a yearly contribution. A simple phone call, a simple thank you note, and acknowledgement from the President of the Norwayne Alumni has helped enhance bringing a family together in so many supportive ways. Finally, I can say, I am proud to be a part of an organization and finally I feel welcome. So, like the movie, *Welcome Home Roscoe Jenkins*, welcome home for me came in 2012.

SAY WHAT? SAY WHAT?